GW00771156

FRENCH HOME COOKING

By the same author:

THE CUISINE OF PAUL BOCUSE

FRENCH
HOME
COOKING

An Introduction to
Classic French Cooking

PAUL BOCUSE

Translated, adapted, and with editors' notes by
Philip and Mary Hyman

GRANADA
London Toronto Sydney New York

Granada Publishing Limited
8 Grafton Street, London W1X 3LA

Published by Granada Publishing 1983

Originally published in France as *Bocuse dans votre cuisine*
by Flammarion et Cie, Paris

Copyright © 1982 by Flammarion
This translation © 1982 by Random House, Inc.

British Library Cataloguing in Publication Data

Bocuse, Paul
    French home cooking.
    1. Cookery, French
    I. Title   II. Bocuse dans votre cuisine. English
    641.5944   TX719

ISBN 0-246-11954-3

Photoset by CG Graphic Services, Aylesbury, Bucks
Printed in Italy.

All rights reserved. No part of this publication may be
reproduced, stored in a retrieval system, or transmitted,
in any form or by any means, electronic, mechanical,
photocopying, recording or otherwise, without the prior
permission of the publishers.

To the women I love . . .

TABLE OF CONTENTS

LIST OF ILLUSTRATIONS

INTRODUCTION
by Paul Bocuse

No truffles, no caviar, no foie gras, no lobster – you won't find any such costly ingredients in the recipes I've written for this book. I've wanted to write a book like this for many years – a book for people who love good food but confess that they've never learned to cook properly.

Good cooking doesn't mean complicated recipes or expensive ingredients. The simpler the food the better, in my opinion. When I'm at home with my family, there's nothing I like better than making leek and potato soup and roasting a chicken for dinner. It's this kind of simple food that is the subject of this new book. I wanted to include recipes that everyone, even the most inexperienced cook, could make. Dishes that are often quickly prepared and inexpensive as well – in other words, that could make up *your* family's meals just as they do mine. I've cooked these recipes, not in my restaurant kitchen, but in my home, using standard household appliances and as few utensils as possible. The recipes are written in a clear, direct manner and are as easy to understand as they are to prepare. I hope this book will "demystify" French cooking and show that there's nothing "magical" about preparing a good meal. Cooking should be enjoyable and relaxing; one of the pleasures of life is a nice meal with friends or family – nothing fancy, just good food.

In my first book, there were many more recipes than there are here (over a thousand in all): classics in the great tradition of French cuisine and specialities from my restaurant. Although a variety of people have enjoyed using it, that book was written with an eye to the experienced cook, whether amateur or professional. This time I've limited myself to about 200 recipes – why? Because I wanted to include only recipes that were simple and could be made without difficulty any day of the week – everyday cooking at its best. I believe that a small and varied group of recipes is better for learning since it allows the beginner to experiment with different techniques and quickly become acquainted with everything from soups to sauces. The list of recipes could have been much longer, and in the future, in fact, I hope to add to it with more recipes in another book.

I've omitted sample menus from this book since I feel that people should construct dinners in the manner that best suits them, but I have included a description of what we in Lyons call a "*mâchon*" – only translatable as "brunch" in English – it's a custom I like very much.

A word about dinner parties here is not out of order. Personally, I think the ideal number for dinner parties is seven people. I'd suggest that you try to invite no more than eight or ten people at a time: if you have more than that the food might suffer (unless, of course, you make a one-dish dinner like the French Boiled Dinner).

Also, don't use your guests as "guinea pigs" and serve them dishes you've never cooked before. Serve dishes which you feel you've mastered and are familiar with – that way, you and everyone else will be more relaxed and enjoy the meal.

Here, as I did in my first book, I can't emphasize too much how important it is that you use top quality fresh ingredients only. Any dish will always be better if it's made with first-rate products.

Lastly, I've included advice on kitchen equipment and organization so that everything will be made as easy for you as possible. In addition, I've seen to it that this book was well illustrated so you can see exactly how the food is served – and to whet your appetite.

I've done all I can, now it's up to you; if you carefully follow the advice you'll find here, good cooking should no longer be a problem. Enjoy yourself and – *Bonne cuisine*.

THE KITCHEN AND KITCHEN APPLIANCES

The neater and more organized a kitchen is, the easier cooking becomes. Here are some ideas on how to organize your kitchen.

Serving dishes and plates should be stored in cabinets within arm's reach so that they can be easily reached. Glasses and coffee cups can be kept higher up (about eye level) in the same cabinet.

Pots and pans, baking dishes, etc. should be stored in the bottom of the cabinet, and extra supplies like sugar, flour or oil in the very top.

Cleaning products can be kept under the sink (some products, which should be kept out of the reach of children, should be kept in a locked cabinet).

The two main appliances are the stove and the refrigerator. They should be kept clean.

Defrost the refrigerator once a month, and clean it thoroughly about every three months (remove all the food and wash the walls with a little warm soapy water, rinse, then wipe dry).

Many stoves have self-cleaning ovens these days; nonetheless, it's a good idea to wipe them clean every once in a while using a sponge and soapy water, then rinse and wipe dry. I personally prefer gas stoves to electric ones, but if you are used to them, electric stoves produce equally good results.

A few smaller appliances can also be very useful, especially a heavy-duty blender or food processor. An electric mixer can also come in handy, although I generally prefer using a wire whisk.

UTENSILS

I'm not one for accumulating lots of "gadgets". What's important is to have high-quality equipment that you really *use* and not lots of bric-a-brac that simply takes up space. A well equipped kitchen should (ideally) contain the following utensils:

Saucepans: 4 in a series, ranging in diameter from about 8 inches (20 cm) down to 5 inches (12 cm), with lids. I suggest buying stainless steel ones with thick "sandwich" bottoms; expensive but everlasting.

Cast-iron pots: 3 pots, either round or oval, for making stews and pot roasts: large – 6 quarts (6 l); medium – 4 quarts (4 l); and small – 3 quarts (3 l). Either in black or enamelled cast iron.

Stock pots: 2 large pots – 8 to 10 quarts (8 to 10 l). (Only required for making boiled dinners and stocks.)

High-sided frying pans: 2 pans, one very large – 11 inches (28 cm) in diameter, the other smaller – 9½ inches (24 cm) in diameter, preferably with lids. Thick-bottomed ones, preferably stainless steel, are best.

Frying pans: 2 pans, large – 11 inches (28 cm) in diameter; and small – 9½ inches (24 cm) in diameter. I like pans made of iron (they should be wiped clean, rather than washed. Put a little coarse salt into them after cooking, rub with a towel to clean, then lightly oil before storing).

Baking dishes and roasting pans: 3 dishes, large – 3 quarts (3 l); medium – 2 quarts (2 l); and small – 1 quart (1 l). If made of enamelled cast-iron they can be used as both baking dishes and roasting pans, but if used only as baking dishes porcelain is fine.

Egg dishes: 4 individual dishes about 5 inches (12 cm) in diameter, made of cast iron or porcelain. For baking eggs in the oven.

Ramekins and soufflé dishes: 8 small ramekins about 3 inches (8 cm) in diameter, 6 individual soufflé dishes about 4 inches (10 cm) in diameter, and a large soufflé dish about 7 inches (18 cm) in diameter, made of porcelain or heat-resistant glass.

Knives: 1 large cook's knife, 1 bread knife, 1 serrated knife (for cutting citrus fruits), 2 medium-sized all-purpose knives. Stainless steel knives are the most practical. (Also have a knife sharpener or steel.)

Miscellaneous utensils:

2 wire whisks, a small one and a large one.

Several wooden spoons, a slotted spoon, a fish slice, a spatula, a skimmer, ordinary stainless steel spoons, a set of measuring spoons and a ladle.

A measuring scale and jugs.

A colander, a strainer and a food mill.

A heat diffuser, made of asbestos or metal, to place between the pan and the heat for slow, even cooking.

A rôtisserie (or spit attachment for your oven), a deep fryer and an ice cream freezer.

A vegetable peeler, can opener, corkscrew and rolling pin.

3 pie plates, 8 inches (20 cm), 9½ inches (24 cm), and 10 inches (26 cm) in diameter.

Cake, bread, flan and bun tins as required.

PROVISIONS AND SHOPPING

Your kitchen cabinets should not be packed with foods bought long in advance; nevertheless there are a certain number of things that store well and should always be on hand: sugar (granulated, castor and icing), flour, oil, vinegar, Dijon mustard, rice, beans, lentils, baking powder, pasta, salt (coarse and table), jams, chocolate (semi-sweet), peppercorns, nutmeg, vanilla pods, cloves, cinnamon, thyme and bay leaves.

Try to buy fresh foods only as you need them; too much of even a good thing can lead to monotony, so buy small amounts and vary the meals you prepare.

You should always have butter, double cream, milk and eggs on hand in the refrigerator.

Before you go shopping, check whatever foods you have left over so that they won't be wasted (leftover meat can be used for stuffings, vegetables for making salads if still crisp; soups if not).

This brings me to the *mâchon* or *petit mâchon*, a typically Lyonnaise tradition. It's a sort of brunch, served buffet-style, usually on weekends and holidays. Anything and everything can be served at a *mâchon* – including leftovers. This is the perfect place for the Rabbit Pâté (p. 160), Family-Style Braised Beef (p. 126) served cold, the Mixed Raw Vegetable Platter (p. 48), or any number of the salads in this book.

Simple egg or sausage dishes can also be "made to order" on the spot, and there is always a large selection of breads (and plenty of butter), hot and cold drinks, cheese, honeys, jams and biscuits.

WEIGHTS AND MEASURES

While Bocuse himself only gives metric measurements here there are both the imperial and metric systems. Always keep to one or the other; do not mix the two. Ed.

Some general rules on measuring might be appropriate here:

Teaspoon and tablespoon measurements should *always* be level, unless accompanied by the word "scant" or "rounded".

If working in metric use a metric teaspoon which holds 5 ml, and a metric tablespoon which holds 15 ml; the imperial versions are slightly bigger.

If you use a measuring cup or jug for some items, "scant" means that the ingredient comes almost up to the line indicating the measurement, but not quite – it should never be more than 1 fluid ounce (25 ml) below the line. "Generous" means that the ingredient should rise slightly above the line indicating the measurement but never more than 1 fluid ounce (25 ml) above it.

DICTIONARY OF TERMS AND PROCEDURES

See also INGREDIENTS, p. 17.

BEAT: When the term "beat" is used, either a wire whisk or electric mixer may be used, unless a specific utensil is mentioned. The term is used most often in connection with egg whites, which are usually beaten until "firm" or "stiff". This means that the egg whites peak and will not slide out of the mixing bowl, even if it is turned upside down. Stiffly beaten egg whites are "folded", not stirred, into other ingredients (see FOLD); they must be used immediately after being beaten or they will separate and become watery.

BROWN OR COLOUR: These two terms are used interchangeably. They generally refer to cooking a food in fat until the surface takes on a golden or brownish colour. Instructions can vary, depending on the degree of colour to be attained ("until it begins to colour", "until lightly browned", or simply "brown. . .").

A food should be browned in a pan large enough for all of it to sit on the bottom without piling up; if this is impossible, the food will have to be browned in several batches. Browning is a preliminary operation, so even if the food is divided into batches to brown, it should all be placed in the pot together to finish cooking.

These terms can also be used in connection with roasting and baking; the meaning is the same, referring to the colour the surface should attain.

DICE: To cut meat, vegetables, etc., into small cubes between ¼ and ½ inch (5 to 1 cm) on each side.

DOUBLE BOILER: A double boiler consists of two parts: a bottom, in which a little water is placed and brought just below the boiling point to simmer, and a top, in which the ingredients to be cooked over the simmering water are placed. It is important that the water should simmer, not boil, and that it should never touch the bottom of the top section.

A double boiler can be improvised by heating the water in a saucepan and setting a mixing bowl (preferably stainless steel) in it (make sure the bowl does not touch the water).

FOLD: Stiffly beaten egg whites (and whipped cream) are folded into other ingredients rather than stirred, to keep them from collapsing. To do this, spoon about a third of the beaten egg whites on to the ingredients they are to be mixed with. Using a flat, wooden spatula (a wooden spoon may be used, but it's not as efficient), cut down through the egg whites to the bottom of the bowl, then lift or scoop the other ingredients up on to the egg whites, giving the bowl a quarter-turn as you do so. Repeat this motion over and over until the two are mixed together, then add the remaining egg whites and continue in the same manner. The final mixture should be perfectly homogeneous, with no unmixed particles in it.

HALVE AND QUARTER: This expression is often used for vegetables, and sometimes for fruits. For long vegetables, such as carrots, it means to cut in half lengthwise, then in half again crosswise, forming 4 pieces. For round fruits and vegetables it means to cut in half from top to bottom, then to cut in half again, making the second cut at right angles to the first.

JULIENNE STRIPS: These are very thin strips about 2 inches (5 cm) long. The easiest way to make them is to cut the vegetable into 2-inch (5-cm) lengths, then into slices about $\frac{1}{16}$ inch (2 mm) thick. Pile the slices up 2 or 3 at a time, and cut them into strips $\frac{1}{16}$ inch (2 mm) wide.

PEEL: Most vegetables can simply be peeled with a vegetable peeler, but tomatoes are peeled in the following way: drop them into boiling water, leave for just 10 seconds, drain, and cool immediately under cold running water. The skin will peel off easily. Cut out the stem. *Do not seed the tomatoes unless the recipe includes this instruction* (when this is called for, cut the tomato in half crosswise, press each half very gently and give a flick of the wrist to shake the seeds out).

Most vegetables, including tomatoes, can be peeled and chopped an hour or two before being used in a recipe, but potatoes should be peeled just before being cooked, because they tend to discolour when exposed to air. Peeled potatoes should not be left in a basin of water – they lose their taste and vitamins.

PREHEAT: An oven must be preheated before placing food in it to roast or bake. Allow 15 to 20 minutes for the oven to heat to the correct temperature. *Never* put food into a cold oven and simply set the thermostat to the required temperature: not only will the cooking time be way off, but generally speaking, the food will dry out (especially when roasting), and cakes etc. will not rise properly.

PURÉE: To crush or blend to a cream or paste, generally in a blender, but a food processor or food mill will often work as well.

Starchy vegetables (potatoes, split peas, etc.) should never be puréed in a blender or food processor: use a food mill, potato masher or wire whisk.

REFRIGERATE: The term "refrigerate" simply means to put in the refrigerator. It should be kept in mind that many meats and vegetables are stored in the refrigerator. All refrigerated foods (meat, eggs, butter, etc.) should be left at room temperature for at least 1 hour before being used in a recipe.

STICKS, TO CUT: Whenever the expression "cut into sticks" is used it means to cut into rectangular pieces about 2 to $2\frac{3}{4}$ inches (5 to 7 cm) long and about $\frac{1}{2}$ inch (1 cm) wide.

WARM (for serving dishes and foods): Any hot food should preferably be served on hot plates or serving platters. To warm them, simply place them in a moderately hot oven for 5 to 10 minutes, leaving the oven door ajar so they don't heat too much. If the oven is being used you can either place the plates or platters in the drawer under the oven to warm for at least 20 minutes, or set them over a large pot of boiling water and cover them with a large lid or another plate turned upside down. All these methods can be used for keeping foods warm as well; this is generally required when sauces using the pan juices are made at the last minute.

WHISK: Whenever the term "whisk" is used, it always means to beat with a wire whisk, *never* with an electric mixer (see BEAT). It is employed especially in connection with sauces, many of which require the use of a wire whisk if they are to be made successfully.

ZEST: This is the thin, coloured, outer layer of citrus fruit rinds. It can either be removed in strips with a vegetable peeler or grated off with a fine-holed grater, depending on how it is being used. When the zest is called for, first wash the fruit in warm water and wipe it dry. If grating the zest, be careful to grate off only the coloured part of the rind; the white, spongy part just under the zest has a very strong, bitter taste.

Whenever possible use fruits that have not been sprayed with chemicals. These are generally available in health food shops.

INGREDIENTS

A Word to British Cooks
by Philip and Mary Hyman

The following is a list of ingredients that occur frequently in the course of these recipes. *Read this section carefully before attempting to make any of the recipes.* A short Dictionary of Cooking Terms and Procedures is also included on pp. 15–16 – consult it whenever you encounter a word, expression, or procedure that is not explained here.

BOUQUET GARNI: This aromatic bunch of herbs is made at the last minute, and in France simply consists of tying together a sprig of thyme, a bit of bay leaf, and some parsley (sometimes celery and leek are included in the *bouquet*). The *bouquet garni* is always removed before serving the dish it is cooked with. It is never large – often no more than a thumb-sized bundle of herbs – but it subtly flavours liquids in which it cooks. If fresh sprigs of thyme are unavailable, you can make a *bouquet* by placing thyme leaves and a bay leaf inside a little square of muslin or doubled-over cheesecloth, tying it closed, and tying this to the parsley, leek or celery. It is by far preferable to use this type of *bouquet*, than to use a pinch of powdered thyme or bay leaf in the recipes given here.

BUTTER: *Use only unsalted butter in these recipes.* Butter should always be of the highest quality, and no substitutes (such as margarine) should be used if you want an authentic version of these dishes.

Butter is often said to be "softened". This means that it has been left at room temperature for about an hour or until it can easily be cut into soft pieces. It's extremely important that butter be sufficiently soft whenever sauces or doughs are being made

EGGS: Unless otherwise specified always use size 4 eggs. If using much smaller or much larger eggs, compensate by using more or fewer eggs than are called for, as the case might be.

This general rule, by the way, does not apply to the recipes in the chapter on eggs in this book, where you can use any size egg you want.

FLOUR: Self-raising flour can be used throughout the book. Do not sift the flour when measuring or when using unless expressly advised to do so.

HERBS: Various fresh herbs, such as tarragon, chervil and parsley, are frequently called for in these recipes. Whenever possible, try to use the herb in question; otherwise, substitute more available fresh herbs rather than using dried ones or none at all! For instance, fresh chives or parsley, or a little mint or basil, could be used in many recipes that call for chervil . . .

LEEKS: Leeks are generally sold with their roots intact. To clean them, cut off the roots, then split the leek lengthwise, starting about a third of the way in from the beginning of the white part and drawing the tip of the knife through to the end of the leaves. Wash the leeks carefully under running water, separating the leaves with your fingers to remove any dirt.

OIL: There are basically two kinds of oil; those that support high heat and can be used for frying, and those that cannot. The first type is generally referred to as cooking oil, the second as salad oil. *Choose your oils carefully*. Tasteless oils are preferable for cooking, as well as for some salads; peanut oil and sunflower oil can be used for both, as can corn oil.

Specific oils, especially olive oil, are sometimes called for. Use only the best, cold pressed olive oil – the results are appreciably better than with less expensive oils.

ONIONS: Baby onions are often called for. These are small onions, fresh or dried, that are approximately 1 inch (2.5 cm) in diameter. Generally onions up to 2 inches (5 cm) in diameter can be used; if only larger onions are available, they can simply be halved or quartered and used instead. Only the appearance will suffer; since the cut onions will not stay together, the dish will look less "pretty" than it would with small whole onions.

PEPPER: Use a peppermill and grind your pepper directly on to foods and into sauces. The taste is much better than that of commercially ground pepper. Freshly ground pepper should be understood whenever pepper is called for in these recipes; black rather than white except where the colour might not be desirable, as in a white sauce.

WINE: Sometimes specific red or white wines are suggested for cooking. These suggestions are always optional, but if they are followed, the wine in question should be French (i.e. a French burgundy rather than a Spanish one). Otherwise, when cooking, use only a wine that you would consider good enough to drink; it need not be expensive or special, but it should at least be palatable.

FRENCH WINES:
HOW TO CHOOSE AND SERVE THEM

by Georges Dubœuf

SERVING WINE

Wine and food are inseparable in France. Good food and good wine should be complementary; they should never work against each other.

Wine should be given the same attention as the food at any meal: a well prepared dish deserves a wine that will do it justice.

In What Order are Wines Served?

Here are some general rules:

● White wine is served before red. Light wines are served before fuller wines. Chilled wines are served before those that aren't. Dry wines (red or white) are served before sweet wines.

● At a dinner, wines are served in the following order: white Burgundy or white Bordeaux before red Bordeaux; red Bordeaux before red Burgundy; red Burgundy before sweet white Bordeaux. In my opinion, champagne is best served as an apéritif before dinner. These are not fixed and invariable rules; I could well imagine serving a light red Burgundy before a powerful Bordeaux from a good year. What's important is to serve young wines before old wines.

What Not to Serve Wine with

Certain dishes simply don't go well with wine. In those instances, it is best to serve water.

● Red wine should never be served with salads made with an oil and vinegar dressing, or anything else seasoned with vinegar; pickles, artichokes, asparagus, shellfish, cream cheese, sweets, and sweet dishes.

● White wine should never be served with salads made with oil and vinegar dressings, or anything else seasoned with vinegar; pickles, vegetables in cream sauces, extra-rich cream cheeses, roast beef.

● I would advise against serving wine with certain desserts (with which few wines are compatible). They are: ice creams, sherbets, fruit salads, and chocolate mousse.

White Wine

● Oysters, lobsters, shellfish, hot or cold fish (except those cooked with red wine), vol-au-vent, sweetbreads, roast chicken, boiled chicken with rice, baby lamb, ham, galantine, goat cheeses, and low-fat cheeses should be accompanied by white wine.

19

● With oysters and shellfish in general, I recommend serving white wines from the following areas: Mâcon, Chablis, Jurançon, Bordeaux (dry white), Alsace (Riesling or Sylvaner), Touraine (dry white), Muscadet, Sancerre, and Burgundy.

● With shellfish such as crabs, shrimp, etc., I recommend white wines from Sancerre, Pouilly-Fumé, Pouilly-Fuissé, Saumur, Touraine, Chablis, Meursault, Chassagne Montrachet, Mâcon, Graves, Entre-deux-mers, Condrieux, Alsace, Muscadet, and Savoie.

● With broiled lobster, specifically, I would serve the finest whites from Graves or Corton Charlemagne, Puligny-Montrachet, or Château Grillet.

● Snails, frogs' legs and other garlic-flavoured dishes should be served with a dry white wine or a rosé.

● Broiled fish can be served with any dry white wine or a rosé from Provence or the Côtes-du-Rhône (e.g. Tavel).

● Smoked fish needs a distinctive wine, one made with the Sauvignon grape or one from Alsace, for example.

● Fish soups, especially bouillabaisse, should be served with a white wine from Provence or Corsica: Cassis, Bandol, or Bellet.

● Foie gras, served at the beginning of a meal, should be accompanied by the great white wines such as the Montrachets, Meursaults, Rieslings, Gewürztraminers, or, of course, a chilled Sauterne.

● "Rillettes" from Tours should be served with wines from the region, such as a Sancerre or a Pouilly-Fumé.

● Sauerkraut calls for a wine from Alsace.

● With dessert or fruit, you could serve champagne or a sparkling Vouvray, or else one of the sweet port-like wines from the south, such as Frontignan, Beaumes de Venise, Banyuls, etc. Sauterne and Barsac go well with pastries, dessert creams, sweet fruits, flambéed crêpes, and tarts.

● Sweet wines from Anjou are best with strawberries or raspberries and cream.

Red Wines

● Lambchops, mutton, beef, poultry, game, starchy vegetables, game pâtés, and cheeses should be accompanied by red wine.

● Sausages and pâtés are always good with young wines from the Beaujolais, Côtes-du-Rhône, Provence, or Loire. With sausages from Lyons, we always drink Beaujolais, of course.

● Boiled pork (*potée*) fricassees, and blanquettes call for light, fruity wines from the Beaujolais, Bourgeuil, or Bordeaux.

● Stews need richer and fuller wines.

● Game, fresh or only slightly aged, demands red wines with lots of character, such as a good Médoc, Pauillac, Pomerol, Côte-Rôtie, Hermitage, Mercurey, Juliénas, or Morgon.

● With venison, which has a very distinctive taste, serve rich, full flavoured wines from Burgundy's Côte-de-Nuits, such as Chambertin, Nuits-Saint-Georges, Musigny, or Richebourg.

Wine and Cheese

In France, cheeses are always served at the end of the meal, just before dessert. This is unquestionably the time to serve a red wine if you really want it to be at its best; but remember, wines have their "favourite" cheeses, and not all wines go well with all cheeses. Here are some suggestions:

● Serve dry white wines or rich red wines with hard cheeses such as gruyère.

● Serve light wines, fruity and dry, either red or rosé, with cheeses like Port-Salut, Tomme, Saint-Nectaire, or Cantal. Light red wines go with the blue cheeses from the Causses or Auvergne.

● Red wines with more body are called for with soft cheeses like Brie, Camembert, and Carrés de l'Est.

● Fresh, unripened cheeses should be served with white wines or rosés.

● Virtually any dry, light wine – either white or red – goes with processed cheeses and cheese spreads.

● Serve dry, light, fruity wines and the less well known regional wines with goat cheeses.

● Only a great red wine from a good year, or a sweet white Sauterne or Monbazillac can match the taste of Roquefort.

Everyday Wines

Finding wines that aren't too expensive to serve as everyday or table wine is always a problem. What should you look for? It shouldn't be too alcoholic, and it should be light, fruity, and easy to drink, without too much tannin. Certain little-known French table wines are excellent value, such as Rhône Valley wines, Côteaux-du-Tricastin, Côtes-du-Ventoux, red wines from Provence or the Minervois, Corbières, the Côteaux-du-Lyonnais, the Côteaux-du-Roannais, or the Côteaux-du-Forêt. Some Bordeaux Supérieurs can be drunk young as table wines, as can wines made with the Gamay grape in the Touraine or the Savoie.

Wine Glasses

The wine you serve and the glass it's served in should be perfectly suited to each other. The glass should be clear to show off the limpidity of the wine. An incident that occurred several years ago is worth relating here apropos of wine and glasses.

I was invited to dinner by some friends; knowing my interest in wines, they had decided to serve a Musigny from an excellent year. They told me before dinner what the wine would be, so it was with great expectations that I went into the dining room. There, on the table, I was shocked to see large blue-tinted glasses next to every plate. At the end of the table was the Burgundy in its basket, waiting to be sacrificed. And sacrificed it was. Not a hint of its colour was visible through the dark blue crystal of my glass. I took a sip and searched in vain for the dimension the glass hid from me, but tasting could not restore what my eyes couldn't see. The glasses were beautiful in themselves – but what a pity to serve a great wine in them.

You, as a drinker of wine, are the last in a long chain that stretches from the vineyard to your table. Your responsibilities are multiple, and one of them should include serving wine under optimal conditions. The glasses you use are of great importance; they should be suited to the wine you are serving, and they should be perfectly transparent and colourless, so that the beautiful colour of a good wine can be appreciated. Any wine drinker who is serious about wine appreciates the way a wine looks and smells as much as how it tastes.

A good wine glass should be sufficiently large, light, well balanced, and plain (not decorated in any way), and the stem of the glass should be plain; any ornamentation is superfluous. The shape of the glass should be appropriate to the wine you serve as well.

● Red wine from Burgundy calls for a big, wide glass, since contact with the air is essential to the development of its bouquet.

● Red Bordeaux are more delicate, fine, and racy; they need less contact with the air, and therefore a narrower glass.

● Never serve Champagne in the wide, shallow glasses that are often used for it – its aroma and elegance can be appreciated only in the tall, narrow "flute" made for it.

● Long-stemmed Alsatian wine glasses should be made of clear glass, even if the stem is coloured.

● Anjou wines have their own glass, made with an almost flat base which gives the glass a squarish appearance.

Whatever glass you use, it must have a stem about 2 to 2¼ inches (5 to 6 cm) long so that your hand won't touch the bowl of the glass and warm the wine in it, and ideally, the rim should be slightly narrower than the base of the bowl. Fill the glass only halfway when pouring wine, then tip the glass and look at the wine's colour. To bring out the bouquet, or aroma, of the wine, gently swirl it in the glass, then smell it for the first time.

Temperatures for Serving Wine

Before addressing the question of the temperature, here is some general advice about serving wine.

● Wine must always be allowed to rest before being served, so don't buy it at the last minute.

● If you've been on a wine-buying trip to the vineyards, don't open the bottles when you get back, or even the next day. Let the wine rest at least 8 to 10 days if it has been travelling. This is especially important with regard to wines 5 or 10 years old or more, if you want to serve them at their best.

Now to the important question of serving temperatures.

● Beware of people who generalize about temperatures.

● Every wine is unique; it differs from others of the same kind by its maturity and whether it was made in a good or bad year.

● In general, wines should be served cool, rather than warm; the rule of serving wine at room temperature cannot be applied to all wines. Whenever wine is said to be served *chambré*, this means it is served at room temperature. Leaving it for several hours in your dining room will generally mean serving it at 64° to 72°F (18° to 22°C). This is a good temperature for young red wines in general, but light, young red wines from Beaujolais or Bourgueil should be served cool, though not chilled – at about 50° to 54°F (10° to 12°C) – as should light, fruity everyday wines. Better Burgundies and Bordeaux should be served at room temperature, as should any red wine, for that matter, 5 years or older.

● White wines need to be chilled, but they should not be too cold. The ideal temperature for serving them is 50°F (10°C). In the summer, without air conditioning, a red wine taken from a cool cellar can be drunk right away, the room temperature having already "warmed" the wine glass. The coolness of the wine in such circumstances is often pleasant. In warm weather, it is best to bring bottles up from the cellar as they are needed, since bottles left in a really warm room too long are not as good as those which are still slightly cool. Whatever you do, don't ever try to speed the process of bringing a wine to room temperature (if you are serving it that way) by heating it, either in hot water or by any other means. Heated wine is not *chambré*.

● Remember, it is better to serve wine cool rather than warm. If need be, you can always slightly warm any wine by simply holding the bowl of the glass in your hand and swirling gently. If, on the contrary, you want to cool wine, simply use an ice bucket; it's the simplest and best way to do it.

● If you refrigerate wine to cool it, leave it for at least an hour or two in the refrigerator before serving, but never leave wines for long periods of time in the refrigerator – overnight, for example – since the cold will damage the taste.

Uncorking and Decanting Wine

Taking the cork out of a bottle of wine seems like a very simple operation, but in fact it can be a delicate one. Don't ever shake the wine before removing the cork; old wines in particular should be handled gently.

The first thing to do is to cut off the seal that covers the cork, just above the little rim on the neck of the bottle. Use a corkscrew that is long enough to go almost through the cork so that you won't tear and break the cork when pulling it out. The corkscrew should not have a tight spiral but rather a wide, open one so as not to bore a big central hole in the cork and damage it.

Young red wines and white wines can be uncorked just before being served. Older reds, and Bordeaux in particular, should be opened at least 30 minutes before being served.

Not all wines need to be decanted. It is rarely done for white wines or for Burgundies. Old red Bordeaux that are going to be decanted should be stood upright for several hours or overnight so that the impurities in the wine will fall to the bottom of the bottle. Decanting is primarily used for such older wines in order to remove this natural deposit (the deposit itself is often a sign of quality in a Bordeaux). To decant the wine, remove the cork, then tip the decanter and the bottle toward each other and gently pour the wine into the decanter. Be careful not to pour any of the deposit into the decanter. Remember that wine should be drunk relatively soon after being decanted. The same holds true for a bottle that has been opened; the wine in it won't keep for a very long time.

THE WINE CELLAR

I would now like to discuss both the buying and the storing of wine.

In General

Even someone with a well-stocked cellar is often perplexed as to what wines to serve with an elaborate dinner. You won't always have, even in the best of circumstances, what might be the "ideal" wine. Sometimes, however, you might lack the wine you need because you had not given sufficient thought to the stocking of your cellar: wines bought by impulse rather than because you really wanted them or knew what they were are the kind of purchase you will later regret. Everyone needs advice when purchasing wines for the first time, so try to find a dealer you can place your confidence in.

Wherever you are, beware of "bargains" or "special offers". Look for the names of reputable wine growers and shippers – this is your best guarantee when it comes to purchasing wines. Various "brands" such as the large houses in Champagne, can be depended upon for quality wines.

Ideally, you should buy your wine from the person that produces it; otherwise, purchase it from shippers and dealers who have direct contact with the producers. You can discuss the wine with them and often taste it before buying.

Try to gather as much information about wines that interest you as you can. Take note of the wines that you like when you are in restaurants or with friends. Stop and taste wine whenever you are in a wine growing region. Ask the advice of friends.

Wine magazines often include much useful information and the addresses of good producers or shops you may not be aware of otherwise. Soon enough, you will find that there are a lot of interesting wines to choose from.

Bottling

When buying inexpensive wine, always have it bottled for you rather than purchasing it in cubitainers and bottling it yourself. This may be a tempting proposition, but often the wine you bottle yourself isn't as good as expected because it wasn't handled properly when bottled. In my opinion, the days of home-bottling are past.

A good wine bottler is hard to find; the profession demands cleanliness, method, and precision of those who practise it. Wine has to be handled with respect when it is being bottled; it is a noble, capricious, and delicate liquid.

It has been said of bottling: "Bottling can make a great wine speak or render it dumb forever". Too often, this operation is carelessly performed; wine must be bottled at the proper moment under the proper circumstances. Wine is bottled properly only if you have followed its evolution from the day it was first made, tasted it often, and waited until it was "ripe" for bottling. Wine that is bottled too young is too tannic, strong, and violent. Bottled too late, wine oxidizes, fades, and withers.

Stocking Your Cellar

The ideal cellar should include a selection of different wines, each with a distinctive character representative of the region from which it comes. Here's how I would stock a small cellar, large enough nonetheless to include the full range of French wines, and capable of supplying different wines for a variety of different occasions, and for different types of food.

To begin with, I would buy a dozen bottles of rosé, either from Tavel (fruity, elegant, and rich), from Provence (lighter, easy to drink), from the Rhône Valley (thicker and warmer), or lastly from Bordeaux.

I would buy wines from the Beaujolais, young new wines that are fruity, light, and pleasant.

I would also buy one of the better "crus" from the Beaujolais, such as Chiroubles or Fleurie – wines with more character, feminine and elegant – as well as a Morgon, Juliénas, or Moulin-à-Vent at least two or three years old (more if possible in better years).

I would, of course, buy Burgundies, but here, selecting them becomes more difficult, since there are so many, and so many good ones. I think you should have wines from the Côte-de-Nuits and the Côte-de-Beaune (in particular Pommard, red Chassagne, and Volnay).

From the Côte-de-Nuits, I would buy Vosne-Romanée, Clos de Vougeot, Chambertin, or Chambolle-Musigny from a good year and two to ten years old.

Among the white Burgundies, I think it would be preferable to own some Chablis, Meursault or Puligny, and Pouilly-Fuissé from a good year.

Bordeaux would not be omitted from my cellar; I would start by buying two dozen relatively inexpensive bottles from a reputable shipper or from a grower in Saint-Emilion or Saint-Estèphe. I would have some very good bottles of great Bordeaux from one of the châteaux: Beyschevelle, Cheval Blanc, Canon, Cos d'Estournel, Laffite, Lascombes, Mouton-Rothschild, Prieuré-Lichine, etc. It's important as well to have some good sweet white wines from Barsac, Sauternes, or Monbazillac.

I wouldn't forget to buy good wines from Alsace, white wines that are generally drunk young (between two and five years old). I would buy them from reputable shippers in the region or directly from one of the many "cooperatives".

Some Loire Valley wine should be included; among the whites it could be anything from a light fruity Muscadet to a Vouvray. Red Loire Valley wines would also find their place in my cellar. I would suggest a Chinon, which can be drunk between two and ten years old – sometimes older – or a Bourgueil, younger and fruitier.

From the Rhône Valley, I would buy some young (one to two years old) Côtes-du-Rhône reds. Wines from the Rhône that have more character and can be kept from two to ten years, depending on the vintage in question, would be bought from Gigondas or Châteauneuf-du-Pape. A selection of the excellent wines from the Northern Rhône valley would not be overlooked: Côte-Rôtie, Hermitage, and Cornas, for example.

Any good cellar should also include a good table wine, which can come from almost anywhere so long as the wine is well made and bought only in good years (a poor year means that the wine will be acid, undeveloped, and often unpleasant, whereas in a good year, the same wine could be fruity and delicious).

Lastly, a good cellar should contain some Champagne bought from one of the many good houses there.

The Wine Cellar

You should be very careful about where you store your wine. Several things should always be kept in mind:

● Wine should be stored in a dark place (light of any kind is bad for it). The cellar should be well ventilated, neither too dry, nor too humid, and be at a temperature varying roughly between 54° and 61°F (12° and 16°C). Ideally, a cellar should be underground and facing north. It should be far from any source of vibration that would prevent the impurities from settling out of the wines as they age.

● A dirt floor, covered with gravel, is preferable to a concrete floor.

● A cellar should be clean, well-organized, and aired: too much moisture can affect the corks and, of course, mould will grow on the labels and eventually make them come off. Fruit and vegetables, or any product having a strong odour, should not be kept in a wine cellar.

● If you can't have a real cellar, wine can often be kept in a closet somewhere in the house. So long as the storage place is dark and has a relatively constant temperature (within the limits cited above), you can use it for storing wine. Some companies now make large closet-like units designed specially for storing wine in houses and apartments. These storage units are quite good and keep wine in excellent condition.

● Wherever the wine is stored, it must be lying down, never standing upright, since it is important for the cork to be in contact with the wine. Wooden or metal wine racks are perfect for storing wine. Alcohol like cognac, however, should be stood upright, so a shelf or two should be left for them in the cellar.

● A well-organized cellar should contain a thermometer so that you can monitor the temperature. Wines from the same region should be grouped together, and they should all be clearly labelled. A cellar book, in which you note purchases and observations, should also be kept. It should contain the name of each wine, the year it was made, the amount purchased, the date, the place, and the price. Room should be left on the page so that on tasting each wine, comments can be added about its evolution, its virtues, and its flaws.

A cellar as I have described it should contain representative bottles from all the winegrowing regions of France. It is a collection, like a library, in which personal tastes are reflected, and in which, inevitably, favourites are found. For the owner, each "volume" has its own story to tell.

The Wine Label

A wine label is the wine's calling card. It is its birth certificate. It tells you where the wine was made, when, by whom, and its shipper, bottler, etc.

Talking About Wine

I thought it would be useful to include a few words about the vocabulary used to describe wine. This section will deal only briefly with this subject, since it is vast and complex.

A specialized vocabulary is employed by those attempting to describe the taste of wine. As with descriptions of music or painting, these terms are often full of nuances and extremely varied, since the sensations being described are so hard to translate into words.

The first thing one mentions about a wine is its general make-up, its body, its finesse. What I call general make-up here is the result of numerous factors, the most important of which is the quality of the year or vintage in which the wine was made. What follows is a list of terms referring to the qualities a wine can have. Each of these "positive" terms is followed by its "negative" counterpart, that is, the expression used to describe the wine when this quality is absent.

In general, wines can be:
firm or flat
clean or rough
hard or supple
complete or unresolved
vigorous or old
fruity or séché
noble or dumb

elegant or stiff
fine or common
light or heavy
full or thin
Wines can look:
brilliant or cloudy
purple or tawny
blackish or brown
sumptuous or light
intense or unenticing
Wines can smell:
lively or sulphury
fruity or bland
delicious or passed
aromatic or faded
The taste of the wine is said to be:
sweet or dry
fat or lean
soft or hard
big or stiff
open or closed
rich or rude
supple or thin

This list is by no means exhaustive; every wine will solicit a specific reaction on the part of the taster and call up images and words to describe them. All wine lovers eventually develop a vocabulary to describe the sensations perceived.

CONCLUSION

I have tried here to give you some basic notions about French wines. I could have added chapters about wine-making methods and grape varieties for every region of France, with lists of the specific appellations, but this, I thought, was not the place for such an undertaking. I wanted to limit myself to basic information which would help the reader choose French wines to go with these recipes by Paul Bocuse.

In closing, I would like to remind you to remember all the care that went into making a good wine when you are serving it. A fine dinner depends not only on the cooking, but on the wine you choose to serve with it.

SOUPS

It's always nice to have a bowl of hot soup on a cold or rainy day. Here are a few classics.

SPRING VEGETABLE SOUP
Soupe bonne femme

PREPARATION TIME: 15 minutes
COOKING TIME: 35 minutes

INGREDIENTS FOR 4 SERVINGS:
2½ pints (1½ litres) water
1½ teaspoons (10 g) coarse salt
3½ ounces (100 g) butter
1 large onion, peeled, halved, and sliced
1 large or 2 small leeks, cleaned and sliced
About 8 ounces (250 g) young green cabbage, sliced
2 medium potatoes, peeled and diced
3½ ounces (100 g) sorrel leaves, chopped (*or spinach. Ed.*)
Nutmeg
Salt, pepper

Bring the water and coarse salt to the boil in a large saucepan. In another large saucepan, melt three-quarters of the butter; when it is sizzling hot, add the onion and leeks. Lightly brown over moderate heat, then add the cabbage and stir until it has melted down. Pour in the boiling water, add the potatoes, and simmer uncovered for 30 minutes. Then add the sorrel and cook for 5 minutes more.

Warm the soup tureen by pouring a little boiling water into it, swirling it around and pouring it out.

Taste the soup, add a little nutmeg, salt, and pepper; then pour it into the tureen. Stir the remaining butter into it and serve.

WATERCRESS AND POTATO SOUP
Soupe cresson-pommes de terre

PREPARATION TIME: 15 minutes
COOKING TIME: 35–40 minutes

INGREDIENTS FOR 4 SERVINGS:
2½ pints (1½ litres) water
1½ teaspoons (10 g) coarse salt
1 pound (500 g) potatoes, peeled and quartered
3 ounces (75 g) watercress leaves (stems removed)
6 tablespoons (10 cl) double cream
Salt, pepper

Bring the water and salt to the boil in a large saucepan; add the potatoes and boil uncovered for 25 minutes. Lift the potatoes out of the water with a slotted spoon and mash or purée them by hand or in a food processor or food mill. Put them back into the water, stir, then add the watercress and boil gently for 10 minutes more. Add the cream, lower the heat, and simmer (do not boil) stirring frequently for 5 minutes longer. Add salt and pepper as needed, then pour the soup into a soup tureen and serve.

COUNTRY-STYLE VEGETABLE SOUP
Soupe paysanne

PREPARATION TIME: 15 minutes
COOKING TIME: 35 minutes

INGREDIENTS FOR 4 TO 5 SERVINGS:
2½ pints (1½ litres) water
2 teaspoons coarse salt
3 ounces (75 g) butter
1 onion, peeled and sliced
2 leeks, cleaned and cut into julienne strips
4 carrots, peeled and cut into julienne strips
2 small turnips, peeled and cut into julienne strips
2 celery stalks, sliced
About 8 ounces (250 g) young green cabbage, sliced
¼ of an 8-ounce (250 g) loaf of French bread, cut in half lengthwise
2 tablespoons chopped chervil
3½ ounces (100 g) freshly grated gruyère cheese
Salt, pepper

Bring the water and salt to the boil in a large saucepan.

In another large saucepan, melt just over half the butter; when sizzling hot, add the onions and leeks, lower the heat, and cook to soften but not colour. Add the carrots, turnips, celery, and cabbage and cook, stirring frequently, until all the vegetables have softened; then pour the boiling salted water into the pot and cook, covered, over low heat for 30 minutes.

Toast the bread under the grill and cut it into thick slices; then place it in a warm soup tureen, sprinkle with the chervil, and pour in the soup. Stir the remaining butter into the soup, add salt and pepper to taste, and serve with a bowl of freshly grated gruyère cheese on the side.

HERB SOUP
Soupe aux herbes

PREPARATION TIME: 15 minutes
COOKING TIME: 30–35 minutes

INGREDIENTS FOR 4 SERVINGS:
2½ pints (1½ litres) water
1½ teaspoons coarse salt
3 ounces (75 g) butter
2 small onions, peeled and sliced
About 8 ounces (250 g) young green cabbage, finely sliced
10 lettuce leaves, finely sliced
20 radish tops, finely sliced
20 sprigs of celery leaves, finely sliced
15 sorrel leaves, finely sliced (*or spinach. Ed.*)
2 tablespoons chopped chervil
10 young nettle tips, chopped (optional see *Note*)
Pepper
Nutmeg
2 egg yolks
6 tablespoons (10 cl) double cream

Bring the water and salt to the boil in a large saucepan.

In another large saucepan, melt just over half the butter, add the onions and cook until they begin to colour. Add all the other vegetables except the sorrel, chervil, and nettle tips, if using. Stir and cook until the vegetables have softened. Then add the boiling water, the sorrel, chervil, and nettle tips and cook at a gentle boil for 20 minutes, uncovered.

Add a little pepper and ground nutmeg, and salt if needed.

Place the egg yolks and cream in a mixing bowl and beat with a whisk to combine. Remove the soup from the heat and whisk 2 ladlefuls into the egg-cream mixture; then pour this back into the saucepan, stirring constantly with a wooden spoon. Stir in the remaining butter, pour the mixture into a warm soup tureen, and serve.

Note: The young shoots of nettles in the spring (or the tender tips of older nettles) are excellent in soup. Gather them yourself, but wear gloves to pick them. Ed.

COLD CUCUMBER SOUP
Potage au concombre

PREPARATION TIME: 15 minutes
COOLING TIME: 4 hours

INGREDIENTS FOR 4 SERVINGS:
3 cucumbers about 1½ pounds (700 g) peeled
Salt
15 walnuts, shelled
2 small cloves garlic, finely chopped
2 tablespoons olive oil
15 ounces (½ litre) plain yoghurt (3 individual yoghurt cartons)
3 tablespoons finely chopped chives
Salt, pepper

Cut the cucumbers in half lengthwise and scoop out the seeds with a spoon. Cut the pulp into little cubes, place in a mixing bowl, sprinkle generously with salt, and leave for 45 minutes before making the soup.

Place the salted cucumber in a colander and rinse thoroughly under cold running water, then spread out on a clean tea-towel to dry.

In a soup tureen, mix together the cucumbers, walnuts, garlic, olive oil, yoghurt, and 2 tablespoons of the chives; season with salt and pepper. The mixture should be thick and creamy, so stir just long enough to mix everything together.

Place the soup in the refrigerator for 3 to 4 hours.

Just before serving, sprinkle with the remaining chives.

SALT PORK AND CABBAGE SOUP
Soupe au lard et au chou

PREPARATION TIME: 2 hours (plus 24 hours to desalt the pork)
COOKING TIME: 1 hour 45 minutes

INGREDIENTS FOR 4 SERVINGS:
1½ pounds (700 g) salt pork
3½ pints (2 litres) water
About 1 pound (500 g) young green cabbage
4 carrots, peeled and cut into julienne strips
2 turnips, peeled and cut into julienne strips
½ small celeriac, peeled and cut into julienne strips
4 small onions, peeled and sliced
2 leeks, cleaned and quartered
Pepper
½ of an 8-ounce (250 g) loaf of French bread, cut in half lengthwise

Although this is called a soup it is actually a whole meal.

Place the salt pork in a large bowl, cover well with cold water and leave for 24 hours, changing the water at least 3 times before cooking.

Place the salt pork in a large saucepan, add the water and bring to the boil. Lower the heat and simmer, covered, for 1 hour. Add the vegetables and a little pepper and cook for 40 minutes more.

Toast the bread under the grill, then cut it into thick slices; keep warm in a bowl covered with a clean cloth.

When done, lift out the salt pork and place it on a platter. Pour the soup into a soup tureen and serve everything at once, with the toasted bread and some Dijon mustard on the side.

If there is any pork left over, serve it cold the next day with a salad and some black olives.

POLISH-STYLE SOUP
Potage polonais

PREPARATION TIME: 45 minutes
COOKING TIME: The first day, 2½ hours
                 The second day, 40 minutes

INGREDIENTS FOR 4 TO 6 SERVINGS:

1¾ pound (800 g) shin of beef
1 marrow bone
3½ pints (2 litres) cold water
2 teaspoons coarse salt
1 ounce (30 g) butter
1 large onion, peeled and chopped
2 cloves garlic, peeled and chopped
2 shallots, peeled and chopped
4 medium tomatoes, peeled, seeded, and chopped
½ small celeriac, or 3 celery stalks, chopped
3 carrots, peeled and cut into julienne strips

2 leeks, cleaned and cut into julienne strips
About 8 ounces (250 g) young green cabbage, sliced
Pepper
1 clove
4 medium potatoes, peeled and diced
1 large cooked beetroot, peeled and diced
4 to 6 tablespoons double cream
4 to 6 teaspoons red wine vinegar

This soup, which could make a whole meal, is best if the beef and most of the vegetables are cooked a day in advance.

A day before serving: Place the meat and marrow bone in a large pot, pour in the water and add the salt. Bring to the boil, skimming off any foam that rises.

In another pot, melt the butter, add the onion, garlic, and shallots. Simmer for 5 minutes. Add the tomatoes and cook 1 minute longer. Then add the celeriac, carrots, leeks, and cabbage, cover, and simmer for 15 minutes. Add the vegetables to the pot with the meat, as well as a little pepper and the clove. Cook over low heat for 2 hours, then remove from the heat and allow to cool completely. When cold, the soup may be refrigerated.

The next day: Remove the pot from the refrigerator an hour and a half before dinner. 45 minutes before serving, reheat the soup, add the potatoes and simmer for 35 minutes, then add the beetroot and cook for 10 minutes more.

To serve, lift the meat and marrow bone out of the soup and serve on a separate platter. Put a tablespoon of cream into each soup bowl as well as a teaspoon of vinegar. Ladle the hot soup into the bowls and serve, with any remaining soup in a tureen, and the platter of meat on the side.

CREAM OF ASPARAGUS SOUP
Velouté d'asperges

PREPARATION TIME: 15 minutes
COOKING TIME: 25–30 minutes

INGREDIENTS FOR 4 SERVINGS:
1¼ pounds (600 g) asparagus
1¾ pints (1 litre) water
1 teaspoon coarse salt
1 medium onion, peeled (whole)
4 sprigs of parsley (tied in a bunch)
1 tablespoon cornflour
2 tablespoons water
2 ounces (50 g) softened butter
6 tablespoons (10 cl) double cream
Salt, pepper

Take the scales off green asparagus or peel white asparagus using a vegetable peeler (be careful not to damage the tips). Wash the asparagus in cold water, cut off the tips, and cut the rest of each asparagus into slices.

Bring the water and salt to the boil in a large saucepan, add the asparagus, onion, and parsley, and boil gently for 20 minutes. Lift out all the vegetables using a slotted spoon, but reserve only the asparagus.

Lower the heat so that the liquid in the pot just simmers. Mix the cornflour with 2 tablespoons of cold water and stir into the liquid, then raise the heat and bring the liquid back to the boil, stirring constantly. Lower the heat once more, stir in the butter and cream, put the asparagus back into the pot, and cook for 3 to 4 minutes longer. Taste for salt and pepper and serve.

ONION SOUP
Soupe à l'oignon

PREPARATION TIME: 1 hour
COOKING TIME: 45 minutes

INGREDIENTS FOR 4 SERVINGS:
2 ounces (60 g) butter
4 medium onions, peeled and sliced
1 ounce (20 g) flour
2½ pints (1½ litres) beef stock or bouillon (see French Boiled Dinner, p. 118) or water
½ an 8-ounce (250-g) loaf of French bread, cut in half lengthwise
3½ ounces (100 g) freshly grated gruyère cheese (total)
Pepper
1 ounce (30 g) breadcrumbs

In France this soup is a favourite with late-night people longing for something to eat after a big night out.

Melt half the butter in a large saucepan, add the onions, and brown lightly. Stir in the flour and when it begins to colour add the bouillon or water, stirring constantly. Cook over moderate heat, uncovered, for 15 minutes.

Toast the bread under the grill, then cut it into thick slices.

Preheat the oven to 350°F (180°C or Mark 4).

In a soup tureen that you can put in the oven, place a third of the bread, sprinkle with a quarter of the cheese and a little pepper and dot with a third of the remaining butter. Make three layers in this way, then pour the soup into the tureen, sprinkle with the breadcrumbs and the remaining cheese, and place in the oven for 20 minutes or until the cheese and breadcrumbs have browned. Serve immediately.

VARIATION: A richer soup can be made by beating 3 egg yolks in a bowl with a few spoonfuls of double cream, a little port, and a pinch of nutmeg. Whisk in a ladleful of the soup and simmer (do not boil), stirring constantly until the mixture begins to thicken. Pour this mixture into the tureen over the bread and cheese, add the remaining soup and finish as described above.

MINESTRONE

PREPARATION TIME: 30 minutes (plus overnight soaking of beans)
COOKING TIME: 1 hour 20 minutes

INGREDIENTS FOR 4 TO 6 SERVINGS:

3½ ounces (90 g) haricot beans, soaked overnight

3½ pints (2 litres) cold water

4 ounces (125 g) salt pork or slab bacon

2 carrots, peeled and diced

3 leeks, white only, sliced

3 medium potatoes, peeled and diced

2 turnips, peeled and diced

4 celery stalks, diced

4 ounces (125 g) green beans, cut into small pieces

6 ounces (185 g) shelled fresh green peas – buy 1 pound (500 g) if in pod

2 very large tomatoes, peeled and seeded

2 cloves garlic, peeled and finely chopped

12 fresh basil leaves, finely chopped

4 tablespoons olive oil

3½ ounces (100 g) spaghetti, broken into small pieces

Salt, pepper

A bowl of freshly grated parmesan or gruyère cheese

Put the soaked beans in the cold water, bring to the boil, and simmer for 45 minutes before adding the other ingredients.

(If using salt pork, soak it in cold water for 1½ hours before making the soup – bacon need not be soaked. Cut the salt pork or bacon into small cubes.)

Add the carrots, leeks, and salt pork or bacon to the beans. Cover and cook for 40 minutes, then add the potatoes, turnips, and celery. 15 minutes later, add the green beans and peas, then cook for 15 minutes more.

While the soup is cooking, place the tomatoes in a bowl, crush them with a fork and mix them with the garlic, basil, and olive oil. Reserve.

Spoon a ladleful of soup into the tomato mixture, stir well, then pour back into the soup. Add the spaghetti and finish cooking, uncovered, for 10 minutes. Taste for salt and pepper, then pour the soup into a warm soup tureen and serve, with the bowl of grated cheese on the side.

GAZPACHO

PREPARATION TIME: 20 minutes
COOLING TIME: 4 hours

INGREDIENTS FOR 4 SERVINGS:
1¾ pounds (800 g) tomatoes, peeled, seeded, and chopped
1 large onion, peeled and finely chopped
2 cloves garlic, peeled and finely chopped
1 sweet red pepper, seeded and chopped
1½ cucumbers, peeled, seeded and diced (see Cold Cucumber Soup p. 33)
Salt, pepper
18 fluid ounces (½ litre) cold water
2 tablespoons olive oil
1 tablespoon red wine vinegar
10 ice cubes
10 to 12 slices of French bread, or squares of ordinary bread (optional)
2 tablespoons olive oil for browning bread

Place all the vegetables in a large mixing bowl, season generously with salt and pepper and add the water. Purée in a blender or food processor – this will have to be done in several batches. Pour each batch of puréed ingredients into a soup tureen. When done, whisk the olive oil and vinegar into the soup, taste for salt and pepper, and place the tureen in the refrigerator for 3 to 4 hours to chill before serving.

To serve, coarsely crush the ice cubes by wrapping them in a tea-towel and hitting them with a rolling pin. Add to the soup and serve.

If you like, make croutons by browning the bread in the olive oil, and serve them on the side.

LEEK AND POTATO SOUP
Soupe poireaux-pommes de terre

PREPARATION TIME: 10 minutes
COOKING TIME: 25 minutes

INGREDIENTS FOR 4 SERVINGS:
2½ pints (1½ litres) water
1½ teaspoons coarse salt
1 ounce (30 g) butter
4 medium leeks, cleaned and diced
1 pound (500 g) potatoes, peeled and diced
6 tablespoons (10 cl) double cream
Pepper

In a large saucepan, bring the water and salt to the boil.

In another large saucepan, melt the butter, add the leeks and simmer until they have softened completely. Pour in the boiling water, add the potatoes, and cook uncovered over moderate heat for 20 minutes. Then stir in the cream, add a little pepper, cook 5 minutes more, and serve.

VARIATION: In Lyons we make a version of this soup using a local preparation called *"couennes cuites en paquets"* – you can make something similar by buying large pieces of fresh pork rind and cutting it into strips about 16 inches (40 cm) long and 2 inches (5 cm) wide. Fold each piece in 4, like an accordion, then tie kitchen string tightly around the middle; the result will be the size and shape of a bow tie (in fact, in Lyons we call bow ties *"paquets de couennes"*). Add two of these *"paquets"* to the soup 10 minutes before it has finished cooking. Serve them in a separate bowl with a little of the soup to keep them warm, and eat them with black olives and mustard. (If making the soup this way, don't add the cream.)

Note: The pork rind that can be bought in Lyons is fresh but precooked. Since this will be unavailable in Britain, use the pork rind that has cooked in the Boiled Pork Dinner (p. 136), or simply place it in cold water, bring just to the boil, and poach for 1½ hours. Allow it to cool, then cut, tie, and cook it in the soup as described above (when tying, be careful not to allow the string to cut the rind). Ed.

Leek and Potato Soup

CREAM OF OYSTER SOUP
Velouté aux huîtres

PREPARATION TIME: 15 minutes
COOKING TIME: about 20 minutes

INGREDIENTS FOR 4 SERVINGS:
1½ ounces (40 g) butter
1 pound (500 g) potatoes, peeled and diced
1 pound (500 g) leeks, cleaned and diced
2½ pints (1½ litres) hot water
16 oysters in their shells
6 tablespoons (10 cl) double cream
Salt, pepper
3 tablespoons chopped chervil

Heat the butter in a large saucepan: when it begins to foam, add the leeks and potatoes, and stir over moderate heat until the leeks have softened. Add the hot water, cover, and simmer for 20 minutes.

Place a sieve over a bowl, line with a doubled-over piece of cheese cloth, and open the oysters over the sieve to strain and catch their liquid. Place the oysters in a small saucepan with their strained liquid and bring just barely to the boil, then remove from the heat, lift the oysters out of the liquid and reserve. Check the oysters to be sure there are no bits of shell caught in them.

Strain the oyster liquid into the soup, then purée the soup in a blender or food processor – this will have to be done in several batches. Blend the cream into the last batch.

Place the blended soup back in the pot, taste for salt and pepper, and heat until very hot but not boiling. Place 4 oysters in each warm soup plate and pour the hot soup over them. Sprinkle with a little pepper and the chervil, and serve.

2

STARTERS AND LIGHT MEALS

It's always nicer to start a meal with a small first course than to plunge right into the main dish. Some of the following dishes, however, such as Poached Sausage with Warm Potato Salad, the quiches, or the Chicken Salad, are substantial enough to make a light lunch all by themselves.

Also, you might try the French custom of eating the green or mixed green salads, seasoned with simple oil and vinegar dressings, after the main dish (before the cheese or dessert) rather than before. It's very refreshing.

ARTICHOKES
Artichauts

PREPARATION TIME: 10 minutes
COOKING TIME: 40 minutes

INGREDIENTS FOR 4 SERVINGS:
4 artichokes
7 pints (4 litres) water
2 tablespoons coarse salt
1 tablespoon Dijon mustard
3 tablespoons red wine vinegar
9 tablespoons walnut or other salad oil
Salt, pepper

Choose only artichokes that are firm and green, not bruised or discoloured. It is best to cook them in an enamelled or stainless steel pan to avoid discoloration while they cook. Bring the water and salt to the boil.

Cut the stem off each artichoke, then rinse in hot water before placing them in the pot to cook. The artichokes should simmer, not boil, for 40 minutes. When done, lift them out of the pot and place them, leaves down, in a colander to drain.

Make an oil and vinegar dressing by combining the mustard, vinegar, oil, and a little salt and pepper.

Serve the artichokes warm with the dressing in small individual bowls.

ASPARAGUS SALAD
Asperges

PREPARATION TIME: about 15 minutes
COOKING TIME: 18–25 minutes

INGREDIENTS FOR 4 SERVINGS:
2¼ pounds (1 kg) asparagus
4½ pints (2½ litres) water
1 tablespoon salt
1 teaspoon Dijon mustard
1 tablespoon red wine vinegar
3 tablespoons olive oil
Salt, pepper
½ egg white

Break off the tough, stringy base of each asparagus; then, if using large white ones, peel them with a vegetable peeler. Small green asparagus simply need to have the scales along the stem removed.

Wash the asparagus under cold running water and divide them into two or three bunches. Tie up each bunch with kitchen string both at the bottom and towards the tip.

Bring the water and salt to the boil in a large pot. Drop the asparagus into the water, bring back to the boil, then lower the heat and simmer for 18 to 25 minutes, depending on size: the tip of a knife should easily penetrate the stem of the asparagus when done. Lift the asparagus out of the pot and leave them on a clean cloth to drain. Remove the strings.

Serve the asparagus warm with a *vinaigrette mousseline*. Whisk together the mustard, vinegar, and oil, with a little salt and pepper. Beat the egg white until thick and foamy, but not stiff, then gently whisk it into the sauce just before serving.

VARIATIONS: The asparagus may also be served cold with a simple Oil and Vinegar Dressing (p. 92), or hot as a vegetable with Hollandaise Sauce (p. 87).

MIXED RAW VEGETABLE PLATTER
Hors-d'œuvre variés

PREPARATION TIME: about 1 hour

INGREDIENTS FOR 6 TO 8 SERVINGS:
1 pound (500 g) new potatoes
Salt, pepper
2 tablespoons olive oil
8 ounces (250 g) green beans
4 eggs
1 small butterhead lettuce
1 bunch radishes
2 small heads celery
1 cucumber
4 medium tomatoes
4 baby artichokes
Lemon juice
1 pound (500 g) broad beans
7-ounce (200 g) can of tuna in oil
1-ounce (30 g) can of anchovies in oil
4 ounces (125 g) black olives
Anchovy paste (p. 92)
3 teaspoons Dijon mustard
3 tablespoons red wine vinegar
9 tablespoons olive oil
Salt, pepper
1 loaf wholemeal bread
Butter

This vegetable platter takes a little while to make, but it's worth the trouble. It's the perfect thing to serve before (or with) shish kebabs or barbecued pork or lamb. It can also be served alone at lunchtime or as a light late-summer dinner.

Boil the potatoes in their skins for 30 minutes, then peel and slice them. Place in a serving dish, sprinkle with salt and pepper, and spoon 2 tablespoons of olive oil over them. Stir gently and leave to cool.

String the green beans, then drop them into a large pot of lightly salted boiling water and simmer for 10 to 15 minutes. Taste to see if they're done (they shouldn't be too cooked). Drain the beans in a colander and cool quickly under cold running water; reserve.

Boil the eggs for 15 to 20 minutes, drain and cool under running water, then remove the shells and cut each egg in half lengthwise; reserve.

Wash the lettuce, remove the rib from the centre of each leaf, then place the leaves on a platter or in a bowl; reserve.

Cut the leaves off the radishes, carefully wash the radishes and reserve.

Wash the celery, place in a serving dish, and reserve.

Peel the cucumber, cut it into thick slices, place in a large bowl, and sprinkle generously with salt. Leave for 20 minutes, then place in a colander and rinse under cold running water. Lay the slices on a paper towel to dry, then put them in a serving dish and reserve.

Wash the tomatoes, cut out the stems, cut the tomatoes into wedges, place them in a serving dish, sprinkle with salt, and reserve.

Cut off the stems of the artichokes and dip the artichokes in a large bowl of cold water mixed with a little lemon juice; shake them about to wash and remove any dirt, drain, and place on a plate; reserve.

Shell the broad beans and remove the little skin that surrounds each bean. Place in a bowl and reserve.

Place the tuna in a small serving dish and the anchovies in another; place the olives in a third bowl.

Place everything in the refrigerator for about 1 hour before serving.

To serve, prepare the Anchovy Paste (p. 92) and make an oil and vinegar dressing by mixing together the mustard, vinegar, olive oil, and a little salt and pepper.

Toast 1 or 2 large slices of bread per person, then serve the vegetables, eggs, fish, sauces, and a dish of butter all at once. Place everything on the table and let your guests serve themselves.

GOUGÈRE

PREPARATION TIME: 20 minutes
COOKING TIME: 25 minutes

INGREDIENTS FOR 4 SERVINGS:
2 ounces (60 g) butter, for the batter
4 fluid ounces (12 cl) water
4 ounces (125 g) flour
3 eggs, separated
3½ ounces (100 g) grated gruyère cheese
Nutmeg
Butter, for the soufflé dish

A *gougère* can be served alone or as an entrée or as an accompaniment to meat, especially roast beef or lamb.

Preheat the oven to 425°F (220°C or Mark 7).

Melt the butter in a saucepan, then pour in the water and bring to the boil. Add the flour all at once, stirring constantly until the batter is smooth, detaches from the sides of the saucepan, and forms a ball around the spoon. Remove the pan from the heat and beat in the egg yolks one by one; then stir in the grated cheese and a little nutmeg.

Lightly butter a 6-inch (15-cm) soufflé dish or four individual ramekins, and place in the oven while finishing the batter.

Beat the egg whites until stiff, add a quarter to the batter, stirring them in with the whisk; then add the rest of the egg whites in the same way. Remove the soufflé dish from the oven, pour in the batter, return to the oven, and bake for 25 minutes or until the blade of a knife comes out clean when stuck into the centre of the *gougère*. Serve as soon as it comes out of the oven.

CUCUMBER AND CREAM SALAD
Concombres à la crème

PREPARATION TIME: 40 minutes

INGREDIENTS FOR 4 SERVINGS:
3 cucumbers weighing about 1¼ to 1½ pounds (600 to 700 g)
Salt
4 tablespoons double cream
1 tablespoon lemon juice
2 tablespoons finely chopped chives
Salt, pepper

Cucumbers are easier to digest if they have been peeled and salted before being used in salads.

Peel the cucumbers and cut them into thin slices. Place them on a large plate, salt, then turn the pieces over and salt again. Leave the cucumbers in the refrigerator for 30 minutes before making the salad.

Remove the cucumbers from the refrigerator, place in a colander, and rinse off under cold running water. Leave them to dry on a paper towel.

Make a sauce by stirring together the cream, lemon juice, chives, salt, and pepper. Place the cucumbers on individual plates, spoon the sauce over them, and serve.

HAM WITH TOMATO CREAM SAUCE
Jambon chaud

PREPARATION TIME: 10 minutes
COOKING TIME: 15 minutes

INGREDIENTS FOR 4 SERVINGS:
4 thick slices ham cut from the bone – about 1 pound (500 g)
1 tablespoon granulated sugar
4 tablespoons red wine vinegar
1 ounce (30 g) softened butter
1 shallot, peeled and finely chopped
1 tablespoon tomato purée
6 fluid ounces (18 cl) dry white wine
3 tablespoons double cream
Salt, pepper

Place the sugar and vinegar in a large frying pan and boil, stirring constantly until the mixture has reduced to nothing but dark bubbles. Stir in the butter and shallot, and cook until the shallot starts to brown; then add the tomato purée and white wine. Boil the sauce over moderate heat for 2 to 3 minutes, or until reduced by half and beginning to thicken.

Place the ham in the pan just long enough to heat through (turn it over once), then place it on a hot serving platter. Add the cream to the sauce, season lightly, stir and bring just to the boil, then spoon the sauce over the ham and serve.

Serving suggestions: This is very good served as a light lunch with Broccoli (p. 180) or Mixed Vegetables (p. 172).

QUICHE LORRAINE

PREPARATION TIME: 20 minutes (plus 1½ hours for dough to rest)
COOKING TIME: 35 minutes

INGREDIENTS FOR 4 SERVINGS:
  For the pastry:
6 ounces (150 g) flour
½ teaspoon salt
3 ounces (75 g) softened butter
2 tablespoons water
  For the filling:
4 ounces (125 g) bacon, chopped
2 eggs
6 tablespoons (10 cl) double cream
Salt, pepper
Nutmeg

Place the flour and salt in a large mixing bowl. Break the butter into the bowl in little nut-sized pieces, then use your fingers to rub the flour and butter together. Work quickly to make a crumbly mixture, then add the water and quickly form the pastry into a ball, working it as little as possible. Cover the ball of pastry with a clean cloth and leave for 1½ hours before baking.

Preheat the oven to 450°F (240°C or Mark 8).

Roll out the pastry on a well-floured surface to make a circle about ¼-inch (5-mm) thick. Lightly butter an 8-inch (20-cm) flan tin, line with the pastry, and prick the bottom with a fork. Place the pieces of bacon evenly over the bottom, gently pushing them into the pastry, then place in the oven for 15 minutes.

Whisk the eggs and cream together in a mixing bowl. Add a little salt, pepper, and nutmeg. When the 15 minutes' baking time is up, pour this mixture into the pastry case, lower the oven temperature to 350°F (180°C or Mark 4), and bake for 20 minutes more. If the quiche colours too much while baking, cover with a piece of aluminium foil.

Serve hot from the oven.

Spinach Quiche (*recipe page 60*)
Quiche Lorraine

CANTALOUPE AND PROSCIUTTO
Melons et jambon de Parme

PREPARATION TIME: 15 minutes (plus 1 hour refrigeration)

INGREDIENTS FOR 4 SERVINGS:
4 small or 2 large cantaloupe melons
8 very thin slices prosciutto (Parma ham)
Crushed ice

Make sure your melons are perfectly ripe. If you keep them in the refrigerator, it is best to place them first in a plastic bag, because a truly ripe melon will impregnate everything with its odour. Otherwise, place the uncut melons in a large bowl of iced water and leave for 1 hour before serving.

This dish can be served in various ways; I find the following one particularly attractive. Place some crushed ice on a large serving platter. If using small canteloupes, cut off the very top of each one just below the stem and reserve. Scoop out all the seeds with a spoon, then place 2 slices of ham around the opening of each melon, pleating it so it will look like a fancy collar coming out of the melon. Place the "lid" with the stem back in place and serve.

If the melons are large, simply cut them in half, scoop out the seeds, place the ham in each half as described above, and serve.

Serving suggestion: This is delicious served with a glass of port.

EGGS MIMOSA
Œufs mimosa

PREPARATION TIME: about 20 minutes
COOKING TIME: 8–9 minutes

INGREDIENTS FOR 4 SERVINGS:
4 hard-boiled eggs
3 tablespoons finely chopped chives
9 fluid ounces (25 cl) Mayonnaise (p. 89)
8 black olives
1 butterhead lettuce
2 very large tomatoes
Salt
1 lemon, quartered
7-ounce can of tuna fish in oil (optional)

Cut the hard-boiled eggs in half lengthwise and separate the yolks from the whites. Put three half-yolks on a plate and reserve; crush the other yolks with a fork. Place the crushed yolks in a bowl with the chives, then add mayonnaise a spoonful at a time to make a thick smooth paste (there will be mayonnaise left over). Spoon this mixture into the hard-boiled egg whites, and top each half "egg" with a black olive.

Decorate the edge of a round serving platter with some lettuce leaves, then place 4 cupped lettuce leaves in the centre. Remove the stem from each tomato, cut them in half, then place half a tomato in each cupped lettuce leaf, cut side up. Lightly salt the tomatoes, then place two half "eggs" on each one.

Crush the remaining egg yolks with a fork or grind them through a food mill, and sprinkle them over the platter.

Serve with the remaining mayonnaise and the lemon wedges, with or without some tuna fish in a separate dish.

RED CABBAGE SALAD
Chou rouge en salade

PREPARATION TIME: 15 minutes
COOKING TIME: 5–7 minutes

INGREDIENTS FOR 4 SERVINGS:
Half a 3-pound (1.4-kg) red cabbage
3½ pints (2 litres) water
Salt
4 tablespoons vinegar, for the cabbage
2 juniper berries
3 tablespoons olive oil
2 tablespoons lemon juice
1 dessertspoon red wine vinegar, for the dressing
Salt, pepper
3 slices bacon, diced

Cut the cabbage into julienne strips, then drop into lightly salted boiling water. Once the water comes back to a boil, drain the cabbage in a colander. Pour 4 tablespoons of vinegar on to the cabbage in the colander and toss lightly, then press the water and vinegar out with a wooden spoon. Place the cabbage in a large salad bowl with the juniper berries and leave to cool.

Make an oil and vinegar dressing by beating together the oil, lemon juice, vinegar, salt, and pepper; reserve.

Cook the bacon in a frying pan until crisp.

When ready to serve, pour the dressing on to the cabbage and toss, season with salt and pepper, then add the bacon, toss again, and serve immediately.

SPINACH QUICHE

Tarte aux épinards
Photo page 55

PREPARATION TIME: 30 minutes (plus 1½ hours for dough to rest)
COOKING TIME: 35 minutes

INGREDIENTS FOR 5 TO 6 SERVINGS:
  For the pastry:
7 ounces (200 g) flour
¾ teaspoon salt
3½ ounces (100 g) softened butter
3 tablespoons water
  For the filling:
2¼ pounds (1 kg) spinach
7 pints (3½ litres) water
4 teaspoons salt
Salt, pepper
2 eggs
7 fluid ounces (20 cl) double cream
3½ ounces (100 g) grated gruyère cheese
Nutmeg

Make the pastry as described in the recipe for Quiche Lorraine (p. 54) but use the quantities given above.

Preheat the oven to 425°F (220°C or Mark 7).

Remove the stem from each leaf of spinach, then wash the spinach carefully in a sink full of cold water. Bring 7 pints (3½ litres) of water and the salt to the boil. Drain the spinach and drop it into the boiling water, boil for 5 minutes from the time the water comes back to a boil, then drain in a colander and cool under cold running water. Squeeze all the water out of the spinach, then chop it coarsely with a knife. Season with salt and pepper; reserve.

Roll out the pastry on a well-floured surface into a circle about ¼ inch (5-mm) thick, and line a 9½-inch (24-cm) flan tin with it. Prick the bottom with a fork.

Place the eggs in a large bowl with the cream and grated cheese, and beat to combine. Season generously with salt and pepper, add a little nutmeg, then stir in the cooked spinach. Pour this mixture into the pastry case and bake for 20 minutes, then lower the heat to 350°F (180°C or Mark 4) and continue baking 10 minutes more. Turn off the oven, but leave the quiche inside for 3 minutes more.

Serve hot.

FISH DUMPLINGS AU GRATIN
Quenelles au gratin

PREPARATION TIME: 15 minutes
COOKING TIME: 30 to 35 minutes

INGREDIENTS FOR 4 SERVINGS:
4½ pints (2½ litres) water
4 large fish dumplings (*quenelles*, see *Note*)
1½ ounces (40 g) butter
1 tablespoon flour
6 tablespoons (10 cl) cold milk
6 tablespoons (10 cl) double cream
Salt, pepper
Nutmeg
1½ ounces (40 g) grated gruyère cheese

Preheat the oven to 425°F (220°C or Mark 7).

Bring the water to the boil in a large saucepan. Carefully add the dumplings and lower the heat. Simmer for 7 minutes or until the dumplings float; this is the sign that they are done. Lift them out of the water with a slotted spoon and drain on a clean cloth.

Place the dumplings in a lightly buttered baking dish.

Make a sauce by melting the butter in a saucepan; when hot, stir in the flour, pour in the cold milk all at once, stirring constantly, then add the cream. Season with salt, pepper and a little nutmeg, bring to the boil, still stirring, then immediately remove from the heat.

Sprinkle the grated cheese over the dumplings, pour the sauce over them and bake for 20 minutes or until they begin to brown.

Serve hot from the oven in the baking dish.

Note: Quenelles are a sort of delicately seasoned fish dumpling usually made with pike, and sold ready-made in France. If you can buy quenelles or make them, it is best to use them, but any fish dumpling can be used in making this recipe. Ed.

RICE AND CRABMEAT SALAD
Salade de riz

PREPARATION TIME: 15–20 minutes
COOKING TIME: 15 minutes

INGREDIENTS FOR 4 SERVINGS:
5 ounces (150 g) long-grain rice
1¼ pints (75 cl) water
Salt
1 pinch saffron
4 ounces (125 g) shelled peas – buy 12 ounces (350 g) if in pod
About 7 ounces (200 g) crabmeat
About 4–5 fluid ounces (12–15 cl) Mayonnaise (p. 89), to taste
20 black olives

Bring the water to the boil in a medium saucepan, salt lightly, add the saffron, and stir. Add the rice and cook at a moderate boil, uncovered, for 15 minutes. Drain thoroughly, then place in a salad bowl.

In another saucepan, boil the peas for 10 to 12 minutes, or until tender, in lightly salted water. Drain, then add to the bowl with the rice.

Separate out the 4 nicest pieces of claw meat from the crab and set aside on a plate. Break up the rest of the meat, removing any pieces of cartilage you find, and set aside on another plate.

When the rice and peas have cooled completely, add the bits of crabmeat. Stir in the Mayonnaise just before serving.

To serve, decorate by placing the reserved claw meat on top of the salad and arrange the olives around it (see photo).

MUSHROOM AND FRENCH BEAN SALAD
Champignons en salade

PREPARATION TIME: 15 minutes
COOKING TIME: 10 minutes

INGREDIENTS FOR 4 SERVINGS:
12 ounces (350 g) French beans, topped and tailed
3½ pints (2 litres) water
Salt
12 ounces (350 g) mushrooms
2 shallots, finely chopped
2 tablespoons red wine vinegar
2 teaspoons Dijon mustard
6 tablespoons salad oil
Salt, pepper

Cook the beans in 3½ pints (2 litres) lightly salted boiling water for 10 minutes, then drain in a colander and cool under cold running water. Place on a clean towel to dry.

Cut off any dirt on the stem of each mushroom, then wash the mushrooms in cold water and cut into thin slices. Place in a salad bowl with the beans and shallots.

Make a sauce by whisking together the vinegar, mustard, oil, salt, and pepper. Pour the sauce on to the salad just before serving, toss gently, and serve.

CURLY-LEAF ENDIVE SALAD
Frisée

PREPARATION TIME: 10 minutes

INGREDIENTS FOR 4 SERVINGS:
1 medium head of curly-leaf endive
8 1-inch (2.5-cm) squares of toasted bread (croutons)
2 cloves garlic, peeled and sliced in half lengthwise
1 teaspoon Dijon mustard
1 tablespoon red wine vinegar
3 tablespoons salad oil
Salt, pepper

Carefully wash and drain the endive then chop coarsely.

Rub each crouton with garlic.

In a large salad bowl, whisk together the mustard, vinegar, oil, salt, and pepper, then place the croutons in the bowl and stir to coat them with the dressing. Add the endive, toss, and serve immediately.

GREEN SALAD
Laitue

PREPARATION TIME: 10 minutes
COOKING TIME: (hard-boiled eggs) 8–9 minutes

INGREDIENTS FOR 4 SERVINGS:
1 medium butterhead lettuce
2 hard-boiled eggs
Salt
1 small can anchovies in oil
1 teaspoon red wine vinegar
3 tablespoons salad oil
Salt, pepper

Carefully wash the lettuce. Remove the thick rib from each leaf.

Peel the hard-boiled eggs and cut them in half lengthwise, sprinkle with salt, and place in a small serving dish.

Roll each anchovy up on itself, then place the little rolls in another small serving dish.

In a bowl, whisk together the mustard, vinegar, oil, salt, and pepper. Place the lettuce in a salad bowl, add the dressing, and toss to mix. Serve immediately, with the eggs and anchovies on the side.

LAMB'S LETTUCE AND BEETROOT SALAD
Mâche à la betterave rouge

PREPARATION TIME: 10 minutes

INGREDIENTS FOR 4 SERVINGS:
8 ounces (250 g) lamb's lettuce (corn salad) (see *Note*)
1 teaspoon Dijon mustard
1 tablespoon red wine vinegar
2 tablespoons walnut or other salad oil
Salt, pepper
4 ounces (125 g) diced celery
1 small cooked beetroot, peeled and diced

Cut off the base of each bunch of lamb's lettuce, then wash carefully and drain thoroughly.

In a salad bowl, whisk together the mustard, vinegar, oil, salt, and pepper. When ready to serve, place the lettuce, celery, and beetroot in the bowl and toss. Serve immediately.

Note: Lamb's lettuce is particularly small-leafed and tender; corn salad is another term for it. If it is not available, try using very young spinach leaves with the same seasoning. Ed.

MY MIXED GREEN SALAD
Petite salade de mon jardin

PREPARATION TIME: 25 minutes

INGREDIENTS FOR 4 SERVINGS:
10 radishes
¼ small celeriac or 3 celery stalks, cut into julienne strips
2 medium carrots, peeled and cut into julienne strips
1 leafy lettuce
2½ ounces (65 g) watercress leaves
10 tender pale leaves from a curly-leaf endive
1 small Belgian chicory
10 bunches lamb's lettuce (corn salad)
1 tablespoon red wine vinegar
3 tablespoons olive oil
Salt, pepper

Cut the leaves from the radishes and discard. Place the radishes in a large salad bowl with the celery and carrot strips.

Cut the lettuce into strips and coarsely chop the watercress, curly-leaf endives, Belgian chicory, and lamb's lettuce; place in the salad bowl.

Make a dressing by whisking together the vinegar, oil, salt, and pepper. Just before serving, pour it over the salad, toss, and serve.

VARIATION: This salad can be as large or as small as you like. You can substitute almost any leafy green salad vegetable for the ones I've suggested.

WARM POTATO SALAD
Salade de pommes de terre

PREPARATION TIME: 15 minutes
COOKING TIME: 30 minutes

INGREDIENTS FOR 4 SERVINGS:
1¾ pounds (800 g) potatoes
2½ pints (1½ litres) water
Salt
1 teaspoon Dijon mustard
1 tablespoon red wine vinegar
3 tablespoons olive oil
Pepper
1 shallot, finely chopped
3 tablespoons finely chopped chives

Wash the potatoes but don't peel them. Place them in a pot with the water, salt lightly, and bring to the boil. Cook uncovered for 30 minutes or until a knife penetrates them easily. Drain the potatoes in a colander, rinse them rapidly under cold running water to cool them slightly, and peel them while they are still warm (the skins will come off easily).

Cut the potatoes into thick slices and place them in a salad bowl. Make a dressing by whisking together the mustard, vinegar, oil, salt, and pepper. Pour over the potatoes, add the shallot and chives, then toss gently so as not to crush the potatoes. Serve.

WARM LENTIL SALAD
Salade de lentilles

PREPARATION TIME: 15 minutes
COOKING TIME: 1½ hours

INGREDIENTS FOR 4 SERVINGS:
11 ounces (300 g) lentils, preferably dark green or tan, soaked overnight
3½ pints (2 litres) cold water
1 onion, peeled
5 ounces (150 g) lean bacon, diced
1 teaspoon Dijon mustard
1 tablespoon red wine vinegar
3 tablespoons walnut or other salad oil
Salt, pepper
3 tablespoons finely chopped chives
1 shallot, finely chopped

Wash the lentils in cold running water, then place in a large saucepan with the water. Salt lightly, add the onion, and bring to the boil. Lower the heat, cover the pan, and simmer for 1½ hours, or until the lentils are tender but not falling apart.

Fry the bacon gently, without adding fat, until the pieces have browned on all sides, then pour off the fat, remove from the heat, and cover the pan to keep warm.

Make a dressing by whisking together the mustard, vinegar, oil, salt, and pepper.

Once the lentils are done, remove the onion and drain the lentils in a sieve or colander. Place them in a large salad bowl with the chives, shallots, and dressing. Toss gently to season, then place the pieces of bacon on top. Serve warm.

DANDELION AND BACON SALAD
Pissenlit au lard

PREPARATION TIME: 20 minutes
COOKING TIME: 7 minutes

INGREDIENTS FOR 4 SERVINGS:
12 ounces (350 g) dandelion leaves
1 teaspoon Dijon mustard
1 tablespoon red wine vinegar
3 tablespoons olive oil
Salt, pepper
7 ounces (200 g) smoked streaky bacon, coarsely chopped

Carefully wash the dandelion leaves. Cut each little bunch in half length-wise, then shake them in a bowl of cold water to remove any dirt and drain thoroughly. Place in a large salad bowl and reserve.

In a mixing bowl, whisk together the mustard, vinegar, oil, salt, and pepper; reserve.

Fry the bacon gently, with no added fat, until brown. Pour off all the fat and add the bacon to the dandelion leaves. Add the dressing, toss, and serve immediately.

VARIATION: Small squares of toasted bread (croutons) may be rubbed with half a clove of garlic and added to the salad just before serving.

Note: If preferred, the bacon can be cut into 4 slices and each slice cut in half. Ed.

CHICKEN SALAD
Poulet en salade

PREPARATION TIME: 25 minutes

INGREDIENTS FOR 4 SERVINGS:
Both breasts from a roast or boiled chicken, cut into strips
1 small butterhead lettuce, sliced
Tender pale leaves from a curly-leaf endive, coarsely chopped
3 celery stalks, diced
2 baby onions, peeled and finely sliced
3½ ounces (100 g) diced gruyère cheese
3½ ounces (100 g) black olives
3 large tomatoes, peeled, seeded, and chopped
3½ ounces (100 g) walnuts
1 tablespoon sherry (or wine) vinegar
3 tablespoons olive oil
Salt, pepper
1 clove garlic, peeled and finely chopped (optional)

This salad could be a meal in itself – it's especially enjoyable on a summer evening.

Place the chicken, lettuce, endive, celery, onion, cheese, olives, tomatoes, and nuts in a salad bowl and chill until ready to serve.

In a small bowl, whisk together the vinegar, oil, salt, pepper, and garlic (if using). Pour over the salad just before serving and toss thoroughly.

3

EGGS

Use only the freshest possible eggs; if in doubt, break the eggs into a saucer before using in a recipe (the yolk should be nice and round, the white clear with no unpleasant odour).

Keep eggs away from strong-smelling foods in the refrigerator; their shells are easily permeated by the odours, which will eventually change the taste of even the freshest eggs.

An hour before cooking eggs, take them out of the refrigerator so they will be at room temperature when you use them.

HAM AND EGGS
Œufs au jambon

PREPARATION TIME: 10 minutes
COOKING TIME: 15 minutes

INGREDIENTS FOR 3 SERVINGS:
1½ ounces (40 g) butter
3 slices ham – about 4 to 5 ounces (125–150 g)
6 eggs
Salt, pepper
3 slices toasted wholemeal bread

Preheat the oven to 300°F (150°C or Mark 2).

Melt the butter in a large porcelain or enamelled cast iron baking dish, add the ham, and brown lightly on both sides.

Break the eggs into a small bowl, 2 at a time, and carefully slide them on to the ham. Continue cooking over very low heat for about 3 minutes, or until the white is about half-cooked; then place in the oven to finish cooking for about 3 minutes. Season with salt and pepper just before serving.

Serve with toast.

BACON AND EGGS
Œufs au bacon

PREPARATION TIME: 10 minutes
COOKING TIME: about 10 minutes

INGREDIENTS FOR 4 SERVINGS:
8 thin bacon rashers, rind removed
2 ounces (60 g) butter
8 eggs
Salt, pepper
4 slices toast

I like to serve eggs and bacon cooked in individual flameproof porcelain or enamelled cast-iron dishes.

Brown the bacon in a non-stick frying pan.

Divide the butter between the individual dishes, melt it, then place 2 pieces of bacon in each one.

Break the eggs into a small bowl, 2 at a time, then carefully slide them into each dish. Salt and pepper lightly. Cook over low heat for about 3 minutes, or until the white is half-cooked; then raise the heat and finish cooking for about 3 minutes.

Serve with toast.

EGGS WITH VINEGAR
Œufs sur le plat

PREPARATION TIME: 5 minutes
COOKING TIME: about 12 minutes

INGREDIENTS FOR 4 SERVINGS:
2 ounces (60 g) butter
8 eggs
Salt, pepper
4 tablespoons vinegar
4 slices toasted wholemeal bread

Preheat the oven to 300°F (150°C or Mark 2).

Use one small ovenproof dish per person. Divide the butter between them and melt over moderate heat. When the butter starts to foam, break 2 eggs into each dish and continue cooking over low heat for 3 to 4 minutes, or until the white is half-cooked; then place in the oven to finish cooking for 3 minutes more. Remove from the oven, season with salt and pepper, and add 1 tablespoon of vinegar to each dish.

Serve with toast.

74

CREAMY SCRAMBLED EGGS WITH SMOKED SALMON
Œufs brouillés au saumon fumé

PREPARATION TIME: 5 minutes
COOKING TIME: about 10 minutes

INGREDIENTS FOR 4 SERVINGS:
2 thin slices – about 4 ounces (115 g) – smoked salmon
1 ounce (30 g) butter
8 eggs
Salt, pepper
6 tablespoons (10 cl) double cream
8 slices toasted wholemeal bread

Cut the salmon into thin strips.

Melt the butter in a double boiler. Whisk the eggs just enough to mix, and add the salmon, salt, and pepper. Pour the eggs into the butter and stir with a wooden spoon until very thick and creamy. Add the cream, stir to combine, and remove from the heat. Season with a little more pepper.

Serve with buttered toast.

Note: Eggs scrambled in this way are not stiff but thick and creamy, almost like a sauce, so you may prefer to serve them in bowls and eat them with a spoon. Ed.

SCRAMBLED EGGS WITH TOMATOES
Œufs à la tomate et au basilic

PREPARATION TIME: 10 minutes
COOKING TIME: 25 minutes

INGREDIENTS FOR 2 SERVINGS:
5 tomatoes
Salt, pepper
2 tablespoons olive oil
5 eggs
5 fresh basil leaves, chopped

Peel and seed the tomatoes, then cut into halves or quarters. Season with salt and pepper.

Heat the oil in a frying pan and add the tomatoes. Cook uncovered over moderate heat for 15 to 20 minutes, or until their water has evaporated, stirring frequently.

Break the eggs into a mixing bowl, season with salt and pepper, and beat lightly with a fork or whisk (the eggs should not be perfectly mixed). Pour them into the pan with the tomatoes and cook over moderate heat for about 2 minutes, stirring to cook the eggs.

Serve, sprinkled with the fresh basil.

POACHED EGGS
Œufs pochés

PREPARATION TIME: 15 minutes
COOKING TIME: 3½ minutes per egg

INGREDIENTS FOR 4 SERVINGS:
2¾ pints (1½ litres) water
1 tablespoon vinegar
8 eggs

Absolutely the freshest eggs are essential here (see comments at the beginning of this chapter). You will also need two high-sided frying pans: one to poach the eggs in, and the other to keep the cooked ones warm in while poaching the others.

Bring 1 pint (50 cl) of water to the boil in a small frying pan with 1 tablespoon of vinegar. In a large frying pan, heat 1¾ pints (1 litre) of water until warm but not boiling.

Break an egg into a teacup, then slide it gently into the boiling water containing the vinegar. Lower the heat so the water simmers but does not boil, and poach the egg for 3½ minutes. Lift it out of the water with a slotted spoon and place it in the warm water while poaching the remaining eggs one by one. Be careful not to break the yolks, both when you crack the eggs and when you lift them out of the water. With a little practice, you will be able to poach 2, 3, or even 4 eggs at a time but if you do, increase the amount of water and vinegar in the first pan (2 eggs can be poached in the amounts given) and use a larger frying pan.

Once all the eggs are poached, lift them out of the warm water and leave for a few seconds on kitchen towel to drain before serving.

Serving suggestions: Serve with the Dandelion and Bacon Salad (p. 71) or with Spinach (p. 181).

BAKED EGGS WITH CREAM
Œufs en cocotte à la crème

PREPARATION TIME: about 10 minutes
COOKING TIME: about 15 minutes

INGREDIENTS FOR 8 SERVINGS:
Butter
7 fluid ounces (20 cl) double cream
Salt, pepper
8 eggs
4 slices bread, crust removed
8 small cilantro (Chinese parsley) leaves

Preheat the oven to 350°F (180°C or Mark 4).

Butter 8 little ramekins; place a teaspoon of cream and a little salt and pepper in each one. One at a time, break the eggs into a teacup, then gently slide each one into a ramekin and top with a teaspoon of cream.

77

Line a large roasting pan with greaseproof paper, place the ramekins in the pan, and pour in enough hot water to come halfway up the sides of the ramekins (the paper will keep the water from bubbling up too much and spilling into the ramekins later). Heat on top of the stove until the water is simmering but not boiling. Place the pan in the oven and bake for 4 minutes, or until the egg whites are opaque.

Toast the bread, butter it, then cut each slice into "fingers" about ½ inch (1 cm) wide.

Remove the roasting pan from the oven, lift the ramekins out, and wipe each one dry. Place two ramekins on a large dinner plate, place a cilantro leaf in the centre of each one, and surround the ramekins with the pieces of toast.

Serve immediately.

MUSHROOM OMELETTE
Omelette aux champignons

PREPARATION TIME: about 10 minutes
COOKING TIME: about 25 minutes

INGREDIENTS FOR 4 SERVINGS:
8 ounces (250 g) mushrooms
1½ ounces (40 g) butter
Salt, pepper
8 eggs

Cut off any dirt from the stems of the mushrooms, then wash the mushrooms carefully and cut them in half lengthwise or into slices if they are large.

Melt half the butter in a very large frying pan. Add the mushrooms, salt, and pepper, and cook over moderate heat, stirring frequently, until all the liquid from the mushrooms has evaporated (about 10 to 15 minutes).

Break the eggs into a mixing bowl, season with salt and pepper, and beat lightly with a fork. Pour the mushrooms into the bowl with the eggs.

Melt the remaining butter in the pan; when hot, pour in the egg-mushroom mixture and cook for 5 to 10 minutes, or until done. Slide the omelette out of the pan and on to a warm serving platter, giving the pan a gentle flip when the omelette is halfway on to the platter so that it will fold over on itself. Serve immediately.

Note: Unless you have a very large frying pan, make two omelettes, instead of one, using half the egg-mushroom mixture each time. Keep the first omelette warm in a low oven while making the second one.

Be careful not to overcook the omelette; it is done when the surface is set and creamy but not yet dry. Ed.

POTATO AND BACON OMELETTE
Omelette aux pommes de terre et au lard

PREPARATION TIME: 10 minutes
COOKING TIME: 15 minutes

INGREDIENTS FOR 4 SERVINGS:
3½ ounces (100 g) bacon, diced
1½ ounces (40 g) butter
2 medium potatoes, boiled and thickly sliced or diced
7 eggs
Salt, pepper

Fry the bacon, without added fat, in a very large frying pan. Cook slowly so that the bacon fat melts, turning the pieces over several times for even browning.

Remove the bacon from the pan and place on kitchen paper to drain. Discard the fat. Wipe the frying pan with a clean paper towel, then melt the butter in it. When the butter starts to foam, add the potatoes and brown over moderate heat, turning them over carefully so they do not break.

Break the eggs into a mixing bowl, season with salt and pepper, add a tablespoon of cold water, and beat with a fork just enough to break the yolks and mix them slightly with the whites; they should not be well mixed. Put the pieces of bacon back into the pan, then add the eggs. Cook for 5 to 10 minutes, or until done, then slide the omelette on to a warm serving platter, giving it a gentle flip so that it will fold over on itself. Serve immediately.

Serving suggestion: This omelette is excellent with a Green Salad (p. 66).

Note: The omelette is done when the surface is set and creamy but not yet dry. Ed.

CHEESE SOUFFLÉ OMELETTE
Omelette soufflée au fromage

PREPARATION TIME: 5 minutes
COOKING TIME: 10–12 minutes

INGREDIENTS FOR 4 SERVINGS:
7 eggs, separated
3½ ounces (100 g) grated old Mimolette cheese (see *Note*)
Salt, pepper
Nutmeg
1 ounce (20 g) softened butter, for the dish
Butter

Preheat the oven to 425°F (220°C or Mark 7).

Place the egg yolks in a mixing bowl with the grated cheese, a little salt, pepper, and nutmeg. Beat with a spoon to combine.

In a large mixing bowl, beat the whites until stiff, then fold a quarter of them into the yolk-cheese mixture using a wooden spoon or spatula. When smooth, add the remaining whites and fold them in.

Butter a medium-sized baking dish, pour in the batter, and bake for 10 to 12 minutes, or until golden brown on top. Remove from the oven and serve immediately.

Note: Mimolette is a hard cheese from Holland not generally available in Britain. Another hard Dutch cheese (preferably an aged one) such as Edam or Gouda, or even a mild Cheddar, could be used instead. Ed.

4

SAUCES

A good sauce should be smooth and creamy; it can be thickened with flour, eggs, or cream. Here are a few sauces that go with recipes in this book as well as with many others.

WHITE SAUCE
Sauce blanche

PREPARATION TIME: 15 minutes
COOKING TIME: 15 minutes (maximum)

INGREDIENTS FOR 4 SERVINGS:
2 ounces (50 g) butter
2 tablespoons (20 g) flour
9 fluid ounces (25 cl) cold milk
7 fluid ounces (20 cl) double cream
Nutmeg
Salt, pepper
1 teaspoon lemon juice (optional)

Melt the butter in a medium-size saucepan (enamelled cast iron is excellent). Add the flour and stir until smooth over low heat; the flour should not brown. Pour in all the cold milk at once, then bring to a boil stirring constantly. Lower the heat and cook at a gentle boil for 8 minutes, stirring occasionally, then add the cream, a little nutmeg, salt, pepper, and the lemon juice if using. Cook and stir for a minute or two more; the sauce should coat the spoon when done.

Serve immediately, or keep warm in a double boiler for later use.

Serving suggestions: Use for making gratinéed vegetables: pour the sauce over cooked vegetables and place in a very hot oven for 15 to 20 minutes to brown.

BEARNAISE SAUCE
Sauce béarnaise

PREPARATION TIME: 20 minutes

INGREDIENTS FOR 4 TO 6 SERVINGS:
4 tablespoons red wine vinegar
3 shallots, peeled and finely chopped
2 tablespoons chopped fresh tarragon
Salt, pepper
2 egg yolks
2 tablespoons cold water
5 ounces (150 g) softened butter, cut into 10 pieces
2 tablespoons lemon juice
1 tablespoon freshly chopped chervil (*or parsley. Ed.*)

This sauce must be made over very low heat, just before serving. If you make it in a double boiler, you are sure to get good results. Use the top of the double boiler as an ordinary pot for the first stage of making the sauce.

Place the vinegar, shallots, half the tarragon and a little salt and pepper in the top part of the double boiler. Place over high heat and boil until the vinegar has reduced by half. Remove from the heat and leave to cool completely before finishing the sauce (you can speed cooling by holding the pot in a bowl of ice water).

Whisk the egg yolks and 2 tablespoons of cold water into the vinegar mixture. Heat a little water in the bottom of the double boiler and set the top part in place.

Whisk in a piece of the butter, then continue adding the rest of the butter little by little, whisking constantly. The sauce should become foamy at first, then thicken as the butter is added.

Just before serving, add salt and pepper if needed, then whisk in the lemon juice, the remaining tarragon and chervil or parsley.

Serve in a sauceboat.

Serving suggestion: This is the perfect sauce for any grilled meat.

82

1. Gribiche Sauce. – 2. Garlic Mayonnaise. – 3. Mayonnaise.
4. Hollandaise Sauce. – 5. Bearnaise Sauce.
6. Foamy Butter Sauce. – 7. Tomato Sauce.

GARLIC MAYONNAISE
Ailloli

PREPARATION TIME: 15 minutes
COOKING TIME: 15 minutes

INGREDIENTS FOR 4 SERVINGS:
1 small potato, boiled in its skin
3 cloves garlic, peeled
1 egg yolk
Salt, pepper
9 fluid ounces (25 cl) olive oil
2 teaspoons lemon juice
2 teaspoons hot water (optional)

Traditionally, ailloli is made using a wooden or marble mortar and pestle (see *Note* for what to do if you don't have one).

All the ingredients should be left at room temperature for at least an hour before making the sauce.

Peel the potato, place it in the mortar with the garlic and pound to a paste. Add the egg yolk, salt and pepper, mix well, then add the olive oil little by little, stirring constantly as when making a mayonnaise. Once the oil has been added, stir in the lemon juice and serve.

The finished ailloli should be about the consistency of homemade mayonnaise; if it seems too thick, stir in a teaspoon or two of hot water.

Serving suggestions: Serve with steamed vegetables or poached fish. Garlic mayonnaise can also be spread on toast and served with olives with drinks before dinner.

Note: Lacking a mortar, you can mash the potato with a fork and crush the garlic in a garlic press, mix well in an ordinary bowl with a wooden spoon, and finish making the ailloli as described above. Ed.

FOAMY BUTTER SAUCE
Beurre blanc

PREPARATION TIME: 10 minutes
COOKING TIME: 10 minutes

INGREDIENTS FOR 4 TO 5 SERVINGS:
2 shallots, peeled and finely chopped
2 tablespoons red wine vinegar
7 ounces (200 g) softened butter, cut into 10–15 pieces
Salt, pepper

A thick-bottomed saucepan that holds the heat is preferable for making this sauce.

Place the shallots and vinegar in a small saucepan and boil until the vinegar has evaporated and the shallots are simply moist in the bottom of the pan. Lift the saucepan off the heat and begin rapidly stirring in the butter a piece at a time using a wooden spoon. The sauce should become creamy as the butter is added; it should not become overheated or the butter will oil. Place the pot back on the burner every so often to keep the sauce warm; stir constantly, removing the pot from the heat as the butter is being added. Once all the butter has been added, beat the sauce with a whisk to make it foamy.

Season to taste with salt and pepper and serve.

Serving suggestions: Serve with poached fish, especially salmon and pike.

GRIBICHE SAUCE
Sauce gribiche

PREPARATION TIME: 10 minutes
COOKING TIME: (eggs) 8 minutes

INGREDIENTS FOR 4 SERVINGS:
3 large eggs
2 teaspoons Dijon mustard
Salt, pepper
2 tablespoons red wine vinegar
6 fluid ounces (18 cl) olive oil
1 tablespoon lemon juice
2 tablespoons finely chopped fresh chives
3 pickled gherkins, finely chopped
1 tablespoon capers

Bring a saucepan of water to the boil, carefully add the eggs, and simmer for 8 minutes. Remove from the heat, drain, and place in a bowl of cold water to cool. When cold, carefully peel the eggs and separate the yolks from the whites. Coarsely chop the whites and reserve.

Place the yolks in a mixing bowl and crush with the prongs of a fork. Mix in the mustard, salt, pepper, and vinegar. Stir constantly and add the olive oil little by little as when making mayonnaise. Once all the oil has been added, stir in the lemon juice, chopped egg whites, chives, gherkins and capers, and serve.

Serving suggestions: Serve with Leg of Lamb English-style (p. 132); French Boiled Dinner (p. 118), hard-boiled eggs, raw tomatoes, or celery sticks.

HOLLANDAISE SAUCE
Sauce hollandaise

PREPARATION TIME: 15 minutes
COOKING TIME: 15 minutes

INGREDIENTS FOR 4 SERVINGS:
1½ teaspoons white wine vinegar
2 egg yolks
Salt, pepper
5 ounces (150 g) softened butter, cut into 10 pieces
2 tablespoons lemon juice

As with the Bearnaise Sauce (p. 82), for the surest results, make this sauce in a double boiler. Do not allow it to overheat; especially *do not boil*.

Heat a little water in the bottom of a double boiler. Place the vinegar and egg yolks in the top, whisk to combine, and season lightly with salt and pepper. Continue whisking and add the butter a piece at a time. Once all the butter has been added, whisk in the lemon juice (more may be added to taste, if desired). Heat for 10 minutes longer, stirring constantly. Taste for salt and pepper and serve.

It is best to serve this sauce immediately, but it may be kept warm in the double boiler, away from the heat, if need be.

A variation on this sauce, called Mousseline Sauce, can be made by whipping 3 tablespoons of double cream until stiff and stirring it into the warm sauce just before serving.

Serving suggestions: Hollandaise is excellent with any poached fish or with boiled vegetables such as asparagus or broccoli.

MUSTARD SAUCE
Sauce moutarde

PREPARATION TIME: 10 minutes
COOKING TIME: 5 minutes (plus time to cool)

INGREDIENTS FOR 3 TO 4 SERVINGS:
2 ounces (50 g) softened butter, cut into 10 pieces
1½ tablespoons lemon juice
2 egg yolks
Salt, pepper
1 tablespoon cold water
1 generous tablespoon Dijon mustard

It's best to use a double boiler for making this sauce.

Heat a little water in the bottom of the double boiler. Place the butter, lemon juice, egg yolks and a little salt and pepper in the top; set over the hot water and whisk energetically until the mixture begins to thicken. Whisk in the cold water. Remove the sauce from the heat, pour into a clean bowl, and leave to cool completely.

Once the sauce is cold, stir in the mustard and serve.

Serving suggestions: A tablespoon of chopped parsley may be added to the sauce just before serving with grilled meats, or a tablespoon of capers to go with grilled fish.

MAYONNAISE

PREPARATION TIME: 15 minutes

INGREDIENTS FOR 1 CUP (25 CL) OR 4 SERVINGS:
1 egg yolk
2 generous teaspoons Dijon mustard
1 teaspoon red wine vinegar or lemon juice
9 fluid ounces (25 cl) olive oil
Salt, pepper

All the ingredients should be left at room temperature for at least an hour before making the sauce.

Place the egg yolk in a bowl with the mustard and vinegar or lemon juice and whisk to combine. Whisking constantly, add the oil little by little (no more than a tablespoon at a time at first, then in a very thin stream once the mayonnaise has begun to thicken). When all the oil has been added, stir in a little salt and pepper. Another teaspoon (or more) of vinegar or lemon juice may be added to taste if desired. If you like a thinner mayonnaise, a little warm water may be added, a teaspoon at a time, until the sauce is the desired consistency.

Mayonnaise should always be made just before you use it; *never* refrigerate it.

Serving suggestions: Serve with cold meat or fish, boiled artichokes or asparagus, grilled or poached lobster.

TOMATO SAUCE
Sauce tomate

PREPARATION TIME: 10 minutes
COOKING TIME: 35 minutes

INGREDIENTS FOR 4 TO 6 SERVINGS:
3¼ pounds (1.5 kg) ripe tomatoes
6 tablespoons (10 cl) olive oil
1 clove garlic, peeled
1 medium onion, peeled and sliced
1 small *bouquet garni* (parsley, tarragon, thyme, and bay leaf)
1 teaspoon granulated sugar
Salt, pepper

The better the tomatoes, the better the sauce, so use perfectly ripe ones. Wash them, cut each one in half, and squeeze gently to remove the seeds.

Heat the oil in a saucepan; add the garlic, onion, tomatoes, and *bouquet garni*. Cook uncovered over moderate heat at a rapid boil, crushing the tomatoes at first, then stirring occasionally with a wooden spoon for 35 minutes, or until the water in the tomatoes has evaporated and a thick sauce is formed. Stir in the sugar, then grind the sauce through a food mill or purée in a blender or food processor. Taste for salt and pepper. If the sauce seems too thin at this point, you can boil it some more to thicken; otherwise it is ready to serve.

This sauce keeps well – up to a week refrigerated.

Serving suggestions: Serve with pasta, white beans, fish dumplings, or ravioli.

GREEN SAUCE
Sauce verte aux herbes

PREPARATION TIME: 15 minutes

INGREDIENTS FOR 4 SERVINGS:
1 egg yolk
9 fluid ounces (25 cl) olive oil
1 tablespoon Dijon mustard
2 tablespoons lemon juice
Salt, pepper
1 tablespoon freshly chopped tarragon
2 tablespoons freshly chopped parsley
1 tablespoon freshly chopped chives
1 tablespoon freshly chopped chervil

All the ingredients should be at room temperature for making this sauce.

Place the egg yolk in a mixing bowl with the mustard and stir in the olive oil little by little as when making a mayonnaise. Once all the oil has been added, stir in the lemon juice and season with salt and pepper. Just before serving, stir in the tarragon, parsley, and chives, then sprinkle the chervil over the top and serve.

Serving suggestions: This is excellent with any cold meat, hot or cold poached fish, or boiled artichokes, asparagus, or leeks.

ANCHOVY PASTE
Anchoyade

PREPARATION TIME: 20 minutes

INGREDIENTS FOR 4 SERVINGS:
4 ounces (125 g) anchovy fillets in oil
2 cloves garlic, peeled
1 tablespoon sherry (or wine) vinegar
9 fluid ounces (25 cl) olive oil
Pepper

Place the anchovies and garlic in a mortar and pound to a paste (*or purée them in a blender or food processor. Ed.*). Stir in the vinegar, then add the oil little by little, beating in each addition vigorously with the pestle or a wooden spoon until perfectly smooth. The finished mixture should be the consistency of a mayonnaise. Add pepper *but no salt.*

Serving suggestions: Serve in a bowl as an accompaniment to the Mixed Raw Vegetable Platter (p. 48), or simply with celery sticks and toasted slices of wholemeal bread, or serve with grilled meat or fish.

OIL AND VINEGAR DRESSING
Vinaigrette

PREPARATION TIME: 5 minutes

INGREDIENTS FOR 2 SERVINGS:
1 teaspoon Dijon mustard
1 tablespoon red wine vinegar
3 tablespoons salad oil
Salt, pepper

Place the mustard and vinegar in a mixing bowl and stir to combine, then add the oil in a steady stream, stirring as it is being added. Season with salt and pepper – the sauce is ready to use.

VARIATIONS: Vary your vinaigrettes by using different oils and different acids: for instance use olive oil or walnut oil, vinegar or lemon juice or a mixture of vinegar and lemon juice.

Serving suggestions: Use with any salad vegetables, or with cold boiled vegetables such as asparagus.

5

FISH AND SHELLFISH

The fresher the fish the better: the eyes should be clear and bright, the flesh firm, the gills red to dark red, and the smell pleasant. Shellfish, such as oysters and mussels, are best from September to April and especially good during the winter months. Whenever possible, buy them in their shells.

COD WITH MELTED BUTTER SAUCE
Tranches de cabillaud au beurre fondu

PREPARATION TIME: 15–20 minutes
COOKING TIME: about 25 minutes

INGREDIENTS FOR 4 SERVINGS:
3½ pints (2 litres) court-bouillon (p. 96)
4 slices fresh cod weighing 2 pounds (900 g)
1 tablespoon lemon juice
3½ ounces (100 g) softened butter, cut into 10 pieces
Salt, pepper
Finely chopped parsley or chives (optional)

Several hours or a day in advance, make the court-bouillon as described on p. 96. Place the slices of fish in the cold liquid, bring to the boil, then immediately lower the heat and simmer for 10 minutes.

When the fish is almost done, place the lemon juice and butter in the top of a double boiler, add a little salt and pepper, and set into place over a little simmering water in the bottom of the double boiler. Melt the butter, stirring constantly. As soon as the butter has melted, the sauce is ready to serve.

Lift the fish out of the court-bouillon with a fish slice or skimmer and place it on a warm serving platter. If using the freshly chopped herbs, stir into the sauce and serve on the side in a sauceboat.

Serving suggestion: This is often served with potatoes that have been peeled and boiled in salted water to which a little olive oil has been added.

BAKED CARP
Carpe au four

PREPARATION TIME: 15 minutes
COOKING TIME: 50 minutes

INGREDIENTS FOR 4 SERVINGS:
2 ounces (50 g) softened butter
Salt, pepper
A 3¼-pound (1.5-kg) carp, scaled and cleaned
3½ ounces (100 g) mushrooms, sliced
3 shallots, chopped
4 tablespoons finely chopped parsley (total)
½ pint (25 cl) dry white wine

Preheat the oven to 350°F (180°C or Mark 4).

Use the butter to grease a baking dish just large enough to hold the carp comfortably. Salt and pepper the fish inside and out, then place it in the dish. Around the fish arrange the mushrooms, shallots, any roe that was inside the fish, and half the parsley, then sprinkle everything with salt and pepper. Add the wine and bake for 50 minutes, basting occasionally. Five minutes before the fish is done, sprinkle in the remaining parsley.

Serve the fish in the dish it was cooked in.

Baked Carp
Bream Provençale-style (*recipe p. 97*)

COURT-BOUILLON

PREPARATION TIME: 10 minutes
COOKING TIME: 15–20 minutes

INGREDIENTS FOR ABOUT 3½ PINTS (2 LITRES):
1 leek, split lengthwise
2 celery stalks
2 sprigs thyme
2 sprigs parsley
¼ bay leaf
Sprig of fennel leaves or a little fresh ginger (optional)
2 carrots, peeled and quartered
1 onion, stuck with a clove
½ pint (25 cl) dry white wine
3 pints (1¾ litres) water
1 tablespoon coarse salt
5 peppercorns

A court-bouillon is an aromatic liquid used for poaching fish. Any fish can be poached in a court-bouillon: pike, salmon, even lobsters or scallops. It can be made well in advance and kept in the refrigerator until you are ready to poach your fish. When the time comes, place the fish in the cold court-bouillon, bring to a boil, then immediately lower the heat and poach the fish until it is cooked (cooking times are indicated in specific recipes). Generally, if you intend to eat a fish or large shellfish (lobster, etc.) cold, simply place it in the cold court-bouillon, bring to the boil, then remove from the heat and cover the pot (the time it takes for the court-bouillon to cool will be long enough to cook the fish).

To make a court-bouillon: Make a *bouquet garni* by tying together the leek, celery, thyme, parsley, bay leaf, and fennel or ginger if using. Place in a large pot with the carrots, onion, wine, water, salt and peppercorns. Bring to the boil, boil gently for 15 minutes uncovered, then remove from the heat and leave to cool completely before using.

BREAM PROVENÇALE-STYLE
Dorade provençale au four
Photo page 95

PREPARATION TIME: 20 minutes
COOKING TIME: about 30 minutes

INGREDIENTS FOR 4 SERVINGS:
A 3-pound (1.4-kg) sea bream, scaled and cleaned
2 tablespoons olive oil
Bouquet garni, made with thyme, bay leaf and parsley
1 small onion, peeled and finely chopped
1 shallot, finely chopped
8 ounces (250 g) tomatoes, peeled and coarsely chopped
8 ounces (250 g) mushrooms, sliced
Salt, pepper
4 tablespoons dry white wine
1 lemon, quartered

Preheat the oven to 350°F (180°C or Mark 4).

Brush the fish inside and out with a little oil, then place the *bouquet garni* inside it. Pour the remaining oil into a baking dish, add the fish, and surround it with the onion, shallot, tomatoes, and mushrooms. Season with salt and pepper, then pour in the white wine. Bake for 20 minutes. Turn off the oven, but leave the fish inside for 7 minutes more to finish cooking.

Serve the fish in the dish it was cooked in, garnished with lemon wedges.

Serving suggestions: Serve with Rice (p. 217) or boiled potatoes.

HAKE WITH CREAM SAUCE
Colin en tranches

PREPARATION TIME: 10 minutes
COOKING TIME: 25 minutes

INGREDIENTS FOR 4 SERVINGS:
1½ ounces (40 g) softened butter (for the dish)
1 shallot, peeled and finely chopped
4 slices hake – total weight 2 pounds (900 g)
About 2 tablespoons olive oil
Salt, pepper
4 fluid ounces (12 cl) dry white wine
6 tablespoons (10 cl) double cream

Preheat the oven to 450°F (230°C or Mark 8).

Butter a baking dish large enough to hold all the fish flat on the bottom. Sprinkle in the shallot, arrange the slices of fish on top after brushing each one on both sides with oil, salt lightly and pepper and add the white wine. Bake for 20 minutes.

Remove the fish from the oven, lift out of the dish with a skimmer or fish slice and place on a warm serving platter. Pour the cream into the baking dish and heat on top of the stove until the sauce just comes to the boil, stirring constantly. Taste for salt and pepper, then spoon the sauce over the fish and serve immediately.

SKATE WITH NUT-BROWN BUTTER
Raie bouclée au beurre "noisette"

PREPARATION TIME: 20 minutes
COOKING TIME: 15 minutes

INGREDIENTS FOR 5 TO 6 SERVINGS:
3½ pints (2 litres) water
4 pounds (1.8 kg) skate
4 fluid ounces (12 cl) white wine vinegar
3 tablespoons coarse salt
4 peppercorns, coarsely crushed
1 sprig thyme
1 small leek, split lengthwise
1 celery stalk
¼ bay leaf
4 tablespoons Dijon mustard
Salt, pepper
6 tablespoons coarsely chopped parsley
2 ounces (60 g) capers
1 tablespoon red wine vinegar
5 ounces (150 g) butter

In a large, wide pot, bring the water to the boil, then add the skate and boil for 2 minutes, a piece at a time. Drain it, place on a cutting board, and use a small knife to remove the skin.

Cut the fish into equal portions, then place the pieces back in the pot. Pour in enough cold water to cover. Add the vinegar, salt, pepper, thyme, leek, celery, and bay leaf. Bring to the boil, then immediately remove the pot from the heat, cover, and leave the skate in the hot water for 10 minutes to cook.

While the skate is cooking, spread the mustard over the bottom of a large porcelain or earthenware dish. Lift the skate out of its cooking liquid with a skimmer or fish slice, and place it in the dish with the mustard. Sprinkle with salt, pepper, and parsley, then add the capers and red wine vinegar.

Meanwhile, melt the butter in a frying pan until it begins to colour. Don't let it become black and burnt – just a nice, nut-brown colour. Pour the butter over the fish and serve.

Serving suggestion: Serve with steamed potatoes.

RED MULLET IN PAPILLOTES
Rougets en papillotes

PREPARATION TIME: 10 minutes
COOKING TIME: 15 minutes

INGREDIENTS FOR 6 SERVINGS:
6 small red mullet weighing about 8 ounces (250 g) each (see *Note*)
2 tablespoons olive oil
Fennel seeds
2 tomatoes, peeled and chopped
3 chopped shallots
4 large mushrooms, sliced
Salt, pepper
1 lemon cut into wedges

Preheat the oven to 350°F (180°C or Mark 4).

Remove the gills and scale the fish, but don't gut them (this would spoil their unique flavour, which is provided largely by the liver). Brush the fish with oil, then place each one on a piece of aluminium foil or parchment paper about 14 inches (35 cm) square. Use a sharp knife to make several little incisions in the sides of each fish, and insert one or two fennel seeds into each cut. Place a little tomato, shallot, and mushroom over and under each fish, season with salt and pepper, then fold and squeeze the edges of the foil or parchment together to enclose the fish. Don't wrap the fish too tightly; there should be a pocket of air above each one to allow the steam to circulate while the fish is cooking.

Once all the fish are wrapped up, place them on a baking sheet and bake in the oven for 15 minutes.

Serve in the foil as they come from the oven, with wedges of lemon on the side.

Serving suggestions: Serve with Melted Butter Sauce (see Cod with Melted Butter Sauce, p. 93), or Mustard Sauce (p. 88).

Note: Other fish can be cooked in exactly the same way, but unlike small red mullet, they should be cleaned before cooking. Ed.

MACKEREL MARINATED IN VINEGAR
Maquereaux au vinaigre de vin blanc

PREPARATION TIME: 45 minutes
COOKING TIME: 20 minutes
COOLING TIME: 12 hours

INGREDIENTS FOR 4 SERVINGS:
1 pint (50 cl) water
2 carrots, peeled and sliced
2 onions, peeled and sliced
Bouquet garni, made with thyme, parsley, and bay leaf
1 whole clove
1 clove garlic, peeled and crushed
8 baby mackerel weighing about 2 pounds (900 g), cleaned (see *Note*)
12 peppercorns
1 teaspoon coarse salt
1 lemon, peeled and sliced
1 pint (50 cl) white wine vinegar

In a medium saucepan bring the water to the boil, then add the carrots, onions, *bouquet garni*, clove, and garlic. Boil over moderate heat for 12 minutes.

Place the mackerel in a deep porcelain serving dish and sprinkle with the peppercorns and coarse salt. Lay the slices of lemon on top of the fish.

Add the vinegar to the saucepan with the water and vegetables, bring to a rolling boil, and pour immediately over the fish. The fish should be completely covered; if there is too much liquid, discard any extra, but place all the vegetables and seasonings in with the fish. Leave to cool overnight (the fish will cook while cooling). Serve cold.

Note: This recipe is for very small fish weighing about 4 ounces (125 g) each. If only large fish are available, fillet them and proceed exactly as described above. Ed.

MONKFISH
Lotte

PREPARATION TIME: 15 minutes
COOKING TIME: 15 minutes

INGREDIENTS FOR 4 SERVINGS:
4 slices monkfish – about 1¾ pounds (800 g)
Flour
Salt, pepper
1 ounce (30 g) butter
1 clove garlic, whole and unpeeled
1 tablespoon lemon juice
4 fluid ounces (12 cl) dry white wine

Roll the slices of fish in flour, then shake to remove any excess. Season each slice on both sides.

Melt the butter in a large frying pan; when it begins to foam, place the slices of fish in the pan, add the garlic, and cook over moderate heat for 7 minutes on each side. Remove the fish with a skimmer or fish slice and place on a warm serving platter.

Add the lemon juice and wine to the pan, and boil rapidly, scraping the bottom of the pan with a wooden spoon, for a few seconds. The sauce should thicken slightly. Add a little salt and pepper, then pour the sauce over the fish and serve.

Serving suggestions: Serve with Rice (p. 217) or steamed potatoes, with a dish of butter on the side.

TROUT OR WHITING MEUNIÈRE
Truites ou merlans meunière

PREPARATION TIME: 15 minutes
COOKING TIME: about 12 minutes

INGREDIENTS FOR 4 SERVINGS:
4 trout or whiting weighing about 10 ounces (300 g) each
Salt, pepper
Flour
2 ounces (60 g) butter
1 tablespoon olive oil
2 tablespoons finely chopped parsley
1 lemon, quartered

Ask the fishmonger to clean the fish by removing the gills and cleaning without opening the stomach.

Season the fish, then roll in flour and shake them to remove any excess before cooking.

Heat half the butter with the oil in a large frying pan. When it starts to foam, add the fish and garlic. Cook over high heat for about 6 minutes on each side, carefully turning them over once with a fish slice (they should be nicely browned on both sides).

Lift the fish out of the pan. Place them on a warm serving platter, sprinkle with parsley and garnish with lemon wedges. Add the remaining butter to the frying pan, heat just long enough to melt, and pour over the fish. Serve immediately.

SMOKED HADDOCK WITH CREAM SAUCE
Haddock à la crème

PREPARATION TIME: 25 minutes (plus 6 hours soaking)
COOKING TIME: 25 minutes

INGREDIENTS FOR 4 SERVINGS:
1¾ pound (800 g) smoked haddock, cut into 4 or 8 pieces
Milk
½ medium onion, sliced
Bouquet garni made of thyme, bay leaf, and parsley
3 ounces (80 g) butter
1 large tomato, peeled and finely chopped
1 clove garlic, peeled and finely chopped
2 small onions, peeled and finely chopped
Pinch of saffron
1 tablespoon flour
4 fluid ounces (12 cl) dry white wine
6 tablespoons (10 cl) double cream
Salt, pepper

Peel off any skin, then place the fish on a platter or in a bowl. Add enough milk to cover, with the sliced onion and the *bouquet garni*. Leave to soak for 6 hours (this will desalt the fish and make it tender).

Drain the fish and pat it dry with kitchen paper. Melt the butter in a large frying pan. When it foams up, add the fish and cook for 5 minutes each side over moderate heat, shaking the pan constantly to keep it from sticking (see *Note*). Lift the cooked fish out of the pan with a slotted spatula, place it on a serving platter, cover, and keep warm while making the sauce.

Add the tomato, garlic, and onions to the pan, and simmer for 5 minutes. Sprinkle in the saffron and flour. Stir to combine, then add the wine, stirring constantly. Simmer very gently for 8 minutes. Stir in the cream and continue cooking very slowly, over very low heat, for 5 to 6 minutes more. Add pepper, salt if needed, then strain the sauce, stirring and pressing on the vegetables to extract all the liquid. Pour the sauce over the fish and serve.

Serving sugestions: Serve with rice or steamed potatoes.

Note: Unless you have a very large frying pan, it will be necessary to cook the haddock in two batches. In this case, use half the butter each time. If you prefer, the sauce may be spooned on to the plates and the fish placed on top to serve (see photo). Ed.

Smoked Haddock with Cream Sauce

SAUTÉED SALT COD AND POTATOES
Morue poêlée

PREPARATION TIME: 25 minutes (plus 24 hours to desalt)
COOKING TIME: 45 minutes

INGREDIENTS FOR 4 SERVINGS:
1½ pounds (700 g) dried salt cod with bones and skin, *or*
1¼ pounds (600 g) salt cod fillets
1¾ pounds (800 g) potatoes, in their skins
Salt
6 tablespoons (10 cl) cooking oil
Pepper
1 whole egg
6 tablespoons (10 cl) double cream
1 large clove garlic, peeled and finely chopped
4 tablespoons finely chopped parsley

Salt cod should be purchased in large, flattened and dried pieces on the bone with the skin still attached. If unavailable, fillets may nevertheless be used. In either case, the fish should be cut into large pieces and soaked for 24 hours, before cooking, in the following manner:

Turn a plate upside down in a large bowl or pot so that the fish will not sit directly on the bottom (all the salt falls to the bottom), and place the fish, skin side up, on top of it. Fill the bowl or pot with cold water and add a few ice cubes; change the water at least 4 times (6 to 8 is preferable) adding a few ice cubes each time. Before cooking, drain the cod and pat it dry with kitchen paper.

Cook the potatoes, unpeeled, in a large pot of lightly salted water for 30 minutes, drain, rinse rapidly under running water to cool slightly, then remove their skins while still hot (they will peel very easily). Cut the potatoes into thick slices or large cubes, place in a bowl, cover, and reserve.

While the potatoes are cooking, cook the cod. Place it in a large pot, add cold water to cover, and bring to a boil. As soon as the water boils, cover the pot and remove from the heat. Leave the fish in the water for 20 minutes, then drain, carefully remove the skin and bones, and break the cod into small flaky pieces with your fingers.

Heat the oil in a large frying pan; when hot add the potatoes and cod, lower the heat, and cook for 10 to 12 minutes, or until very hot, stirring frequently. Season generously with pepper and taste for salt (it probably won't need any).

When the cod and potatoes are hot, whisk the egg and cream together in a mixing bowl. Remove the frying pan from the heat and quickly stir in the egg-cream mixture. Pour into a hot serving dish, sprinkle with parsley and garlic, and serve immediately.

SALT COD LYONNAISE
Morue sautée lyonnaise

PREPARATION TIME: 20 minutes (plus 24 hours to desalt)
COOKING TIME: 25 minutes

INGREDIENTS FOR 4 SERVINGS:
1¾ pounds (800 g) dried salt cod with skin and bones, *or* 1½ pounds (700 g)
    salt cod fillets
2 large tomatoes, peeled and coarsely chopped
Bouquet garni, made with thyme, bay leaf, and parsley
2 cloves garlic, peeled and crushed
Salt, pepper
2 medium onions, peeled and sliced
5 ounces (150 g) butter
Flour
½ pint (25 cl) dry white wine

Salt cod should be purchased in large, flattened and dried pieces on the bone with the skin still attached. If unavailable, fillets may nevertheless be used. In either case, the fish should be cut into large pieces and soaked for 24 hours, before cooking, in the following manner:

Turn a plate upside down in a large bowl or pot so that the fish will not sit directly on the bottom (all the salt falls to the bottom), and place the fish, skin side up, on top of it. Fill the bowl or pot with cold water and add a few ice cubes; change the water at least 4 times (6 to 8 is preferable) and add a few ice cubes each time. Drain the cod and pat it dry with kitchen paper, cut it into pieces about 4 inches (10 cm) square, then remove the skin and bones from each piece.

Place the tomatoes in a saucepan with the *bouquet garni* and garlic, salt lightly, and simmer for 15 minutes, or until the water they give out has evaporated. Meanwhile cook the onions and salt cod.

Melt the butter in a large frying pan, add the onions, and cook until they begin to colour; then lift them out with a fish slice and reserve. Roll the pieces of cod in flour and shake to remove any excess. Fry them for about 5 minutes over moderate heat in the pan the onions were cooked in (the cod should be nicely browned on both sides). If necessary, cook the cod in two batches. Remove from the pan, place on a serving platter, and keep warm while finishing the sauce.

Return the onions to the pan, pour in the wine, and add the cooked tomatoes (discard the *bouquet garni*). Season the sauce with a little pepper, boil rapidly for about 2 minutes, or until it has thickened a bit, then pour over the cod and serve immediately.

Serving suggestions: Serve with Rice (p. 217) or boiled potatoes.

FRICASSEE OF SCALLOPS IN CREAM SAUCE

Fricassée de coquilles Saint-Jacques à la crème

PREPARATION TIME: 10 minutes
COOKING TIME: 15 minutes

INGREDIENTS FOR 4 SERVINGS:
Salt, pepper
1 pound (500 g) scallops (without shells)
Flour
2 ounces (60 g) butter
1 tablespoon lemon juice
4 tablespoons extra dry vermouth
7 fluid ounces (20 cl) double cream

Salt and pepper the scallops, roll them in flour, and shake them lightly to remove any excess.

Heat the butter in a large frying pan. When very hot, add the scallops and cook over moderate heat for 6 to 8 minutes. Shake the pan frequently and turn the scallops over halfway through the cooking time.

Pour the lemon juice over the scallops, stir in the vermouth, then pour over the cream, stirring to scrape any juices from the bottom of the pan into the sauce. Bring the cream just to the boil, add a little salt and pepper, and serve.

Serving suggestion: This is delicious with Broccoli (p. 180).

MUSSELS MARINIÈRE
Moules marinière

PREPARATION TIME: 30 minutes
COOKING TIME: 15 minutes

INGREDIENTS FOR 4 SERVINGS:
7 pints (4 litres) mussels (see *Note*)
3 ounces (75 g) butter
4 baby onions, sliced
4 tablespoons chopped parsley
2 celery stalks, diced
1 pint (50 cl) dry white wine
Pepper
Juice of half a lemon

Mussels should be tightly closed, or should close tightly when scraped or tapped with the blade of a knife (if they are open). If they stay open, it means they are dead and could be dangerous if eaten (don't be afraid, however, if the mussels open and close after being cleaned; they are simply breathing).

Clean the mussels one by one, scraping off any barnacles or mud, and pulling out the little "beard" that protrudes from the shell. Wash them under cold running water (don't let them sit in water), and place in a large bowl as they are cleaned.

Melt the butter in a large pot, add the onions, half the parsley, and the celery. Cook until the vegetables just begin to brown. Pour in the wine, add a little pepper, and bring to the boil. Cover the pot and remove from the heat. Leave for 5 minutes before cooking the mussels.

Add the mussels and lemon juice to the pot, cover and return to the stove over high heat. Once all the mussels have opened, remove them with a slotted spoon. Remove one shell from each mussel, then place them in a large serving bowl (discard any mussels that haven't opened).

Line a sieve with a double layer of cheese-cloth and strain the mussels' cooking liquid into the bowl with the mussels. Sprinkle with the remaining parsley and serve immediately.

Note: 4 litres of mussels weigh about 6 pounds (2.8 kg); other small shellfish, such as clams, can be prepared in exactly the same way. Ed.

MUSSELS IN WHITE WINE SAUCE
Moules au vin blanc

PREPARATION TIME: 40 minutes
COOKING TIME: 30 minutes

INGREDIENTS FOR 4 SERVINGS:
7 pints (4 litres) mussels (see *Note* to
  Mussels Marinière, p. 112)
2 ounces (50 g) butter
4 baby onions, coarsely chopped
6 baby carrots, peeled and coarsely
  chopped
2 shallots, coarsely chopped
1 bottle (70 cl) dry white wine
Pepper
1 ounce (25 g) softened butter (for
  the *beurre manié*)
1 ounce (25 g) flour
7 fluid ounces (20 cl) double cream
4 tablespoons coarsely chopped
  parsley

Clean the mussels as described in the recipe for Mussels Marinière
(p. 112).

Melt 2 ounces (50 g) butter in a large pot. Add the onions, carrots,
and shallots, and simmer for 15 minutes. Add ¾ pint (45 cl) of the
wine, a little pepper, and cook slowly for 7 minutes more.

Place the mussels in a second pot, add the rest of the wine, bring to
the boil, and cover the pot. When all the mussels are open, lift them out
of the pot with a fish slice and discard one shell from each one. Place
the mussels in a bowl and keep warm while finishing the sauce.

Line a sieve with a doubled layer of cheese-cloth and strain the
mussels' cooking liquid into the pot with the vegetables; taste for
seasoning.

Make a *beurre manié* by mixing the butter and flour together with
your fingers until smooth, then break it into pea-sized pieces.

Whisk the cream into the boiling sauce, then whisk in the pieces of
beurre manié. When the sauce is creamy, sprinkle the parsley over the
mussels, add the sauce, and serve immediately.

TURBOT WITH MIXED VEGETABLES
Turbotin aux légumes

PREPARATION TIME: 15 minutes
COOKING TIME: 10 minutes

INGREDIENTS FOR 4 SERVINGS:
1 turbot (*or other flatfish. Ed.*) weighing 3¼ pounds (1.5 kg)
2 carrots, peeled and cut into julienne strips
¼ celeriac, peeled and cut into julienne strips
1 leek, cleaned and cut into julienne strips
2 ounces (60 g) softened butter (for the dish)
Salt, pepper
Bouquet garni made with 2 sprigs thyme, ¼ bay leaf, and 2 sprigs parsley tied
    together
8 fluid ounces (25 cl) dry white wine

Ask the fishmonger to cut off the head and fins, and to cut the fish into 4 pieces.

Preheat the oven to 425°F (220°C or Mark 7).

Cook all the vegetables in a pot of lightly salted boiling water for 7 to 8 minutes, then drain immediately.

Butter a baking dish generously, spread the vegetables over the bottom, and place the pieces of fish on top. Season with salt and pepper, and place the *bouquet garni* in the dish. Add the white wine and bake in the oven for 10 minutes.

Remove the *bouquet garni* and serve the fish and vegetables in the baking dish.

Serving suggestions: Serve with Rice (p. 217) or pasta.

6

MEAT

There is no substitute for quality. This is as true for meat as for fish, vegetables, or fruit. You may have to pay more, but good meat is worth the difference in price. Remember to leave any refrigerated meat at room temperature for an hour before cooking.

ROAST FILLET OF BEEF
Filet de bœuf rôti

PREPARATION TIME: 10 minutes
COOKING TIME: 15 minutes per pound

INGREDIENTS FOR 5 TO 6 SERVINGS:
2¼ pounds (1 kg) fillet of beef, all fat removed
Slices of bacon or pork fat for barding – about 7 ounces (200 g)
Salt, pepper
2 ounces (50 g) softened butter, cut into 10 pieces
4 tablespoons hot water

Preheat the oven to 425°F (220°C or Mark 7).

Wrap the beef in the fat and tie with kitchen string. Season with salt and pepper, then place it in a roasting pan and roast for about 40 to 45 minutes (allow 15 minutes per pound, including the weight of the fat). 15 minutes before the time is up, remove the fat so that the meat will brown. When the time is up, turn off the oven but leave the meat inside for an additional 5 minutes; this will make for more evenly cooked and tender slices (the meat will be very rare, as it should be).

Lift the roast out of the pan, place on a board, and carve, being careful to keep any juices. Cover the meat and keep warm while making the sauce.

Pour off any fat in the roasting pan and place the pan on top of the stove over high heat. Add the juices that came from the meat while carving, the butter, and the hot water. Season with salt and pepper, heat until the sauce foams up, then immediately pour it into a sauceboat and serve.

Serving suggestions: Serve with Potatoes au Gratin (p. 209) and watercress, sprinkled with a little salt and vinegar.

If there is any meat left over, it is excellent served cold with pickled gherkins, black olives, and mustard.

BOILED BEEF AU GRATIN
Pot-au-feu au gratin

PREPARATION TIME: 30 minutes
COOKING TIME: 1 hour 10 minutes

INGREDIENTS FOR 4 SERVINGS:
1 ounce (30 g) butter
2 medium onions, peeled and sliced
6 tablespoons (10 cl) red wine vinegar
1 tablespoon flour
4 tablespoons tomato purée
1¾ pints (1 litre) stock or bouillon (see French Boiled Dinner p. 118)
4 tablespoons chopped parsley
1 clove garlic, peeled
12 to 16 thin slices leftover boiled beef (see French Boiled Dinner p.118)
3 ounces (80 g) breadcrumbs

Preheat the oven to 425°F (220°C or Mark 7).

Melt the butter in a frying pan and cook the onions until soft but not brown. Add the vinegar and boil until it has evaporated completely, then add the flour, stir, add the tomato purée, bouillon and parsley and simmer uncovered for 25 minutes. Crush the garlic into the baking dish and rub energetically, spreading it around the dish. Lay the slices of leftover beef in the dish so that they overlap slightly, then add the sauce, spreading it over the meat. Sprinkle with the breadcrumbs (they should absorb most of the liquid), then place in the oven and bake for 45 minutes.

Serving suggestion: Serve with the Baked Vermicelli (p. 220).

PEPPER STEAKS
Steaks au poivre

PREPARATION TIME: 20 minutes
COOKING TIME: about 15 minutes

INGREDIENTS FOR 4 SERVINGS:
½ ounce (15 g) whole peppercorns
2 fillet steaks, weighing 10 ounces (300 g) each
Salt
1 ounce (30 g) butter
1 teaspoon Dijon mustard
6 tablespoons (10 cl) double cream

Place the peppercorns on a board or table and coarsely crush them with a rolling pin. Lightly salt the steaks, then roll them in the peppercorns, pressing them down hard as you do so. Leave for 15 minutes before cooking.

Heat the butter in a large frying pan until very hot, add the steaks, and cook over high heat for 5 or 6 minutes on each side. Lift them out of the pan and keep warm on a serving platter while making the sauce.

Remove the pan from the heat, stir in the mustard and the cream, scraping the bottom of the pan to dissolve any meat juices, then place the pan back over the heat just long enough to heat the sauce (don't allow to boil). Add a little salt if needed, then pour over the meat and serve.

Serving suggestion: Serve with Sauté Potatoes (p. 201).

FRENCH BOILED DINNER
Pot-au-feu

PREPARATION TIME: 25 minutes
COOKING TIME: 3 hours

INGREDIENTS FOR 6 TO 8 SERVINGS:
2 or 3 marrow bones
A small shin of beef weighing about 6
  pounds (2.8 kg) or an equal weight
  of oxtail and short ribs of beef
2¾ pounds (1.25 kg) veal knuckle
10½ pints (6 litres) water
Salt
Bouquet garni made with 1 sprig
  thyme, 1 bay leaf, 5 sprigs parsley
  tied together
1 onion, peeled and stuck with a clove
5 peppercorns
4 medium carrots, peeled
4 medium turnips, peeled
Heart of 1 head of celery, split
  lengthwise
4 leeks, cleaned and tied in a bunch
Toast (for the marrow)
Pickled gherkins
Dijon mustard
Coarse sea salt

Wrap the marrow bones in a piece of cheese-cloth and tie the ends together to seal them inside. Reserve until required (see *Note*).

Place the beef and veal in a large pot, add the cold water (the meat should be covered) and the salt, and bring to the boil. Skim off any foam that surfaces using a skimmer or slotted spoon.

When the water boils add the *bouquet garni*, the onion stuck with a clove and the peppercorns. Lower the heat and simmer uncovered for at least 3 hours, adding the vegetables 45 minutes before the end.

To serve lift the beef and veal out of the pot and place on a hot serving platter with the vegetables and marrow bones around them. Serve with toast (to spread the marrow on), pickled gherkins, Dijon mustard and a bowl of coarse sea salt on the side.

Serving suggestion: Serve the meat and vegetables with a Risotto (p. 221) made with the bouillon.

On a cold winter's night, serve a bowl of the hot bouillon as a first course (salt and pepper to taste). Whether or not you serve the bouillon, save it, since it is invaluable in making various soups, sauces and stews. To keep the bouillon, pour it into a large bowl to cool overnight, then use a spoon to remove the layer of fat that will have formed on the surface. You can keep the bouillon for several days in the refrigerator.

Note: The veal and marrow bones don't really need to cook as long as the beef. The veal can be added after 2 hours, and the marrow bones can be added at the same time as the vegetables.

Save any leftover meat for making the Boiled Beef au Gratin (p. 116), the Stuffed Cabbage, Tomatoes, or Courgettes (pp. 175, 182 and 188) or the French Shepherd's Pie (p. 212). Ed.

BURGUNDIAN BEEF STEW
Bœuf bourguignon

PREPARATION TIME: 20 minutes
COOKING TIME: 3 hours

INGREDIENTS FOR 4 SERVINGS:
2⅓ pounds (1 kg) blade or chuck steak
4 ounces (125 g) bacon
Bouquet garni made with 2 celery stalks, 1 sprig thyme, 4 sprigs parsley, and 1
  bay leaf tied together
2 ounces (60 g) butter
12 baby onions, peeled
Salt, pepper
4 carrots, peeled, halved lengthwise, and quartered
½ ounce (15 g) flour
1 generous teaspoon tomato purée
1 bottle red wine
2 small cloves garlic, peeled and crushed

Cut the meat into egg-sized pieces and the bacon into ½-inch (1 cm) cubes.

Melt the butter in a large cast-iron pot, add the onions and bacon, and cook over moderate heat for 3 minutes, or until they begin to brown. Season the meat with salt and pepper, then add it to the pot and brown over high heat on all sides. Lower the heat, add the carrots and *bouquet garni*, cover, and simmer for 20 minutes; then lift the meat and bacon out of the pot with a slotted spoon. Stir the flour into the pot and heat until it starts to colour. Stir in the tomato purée then add the wine little by little, stirring constantly. Add more salt and pepper and the garlic and bring to the boil, stirring constantly. Return the meat and bacon back to the pot, cover, and simmer for 2½ hours. Remove the *bouquet garni*, then serve the stew in the pot.

Serving suggestions: Serve with steamed potatoes or a Potato Crêpe (p. 205).

HUNGARIAN GOULASH
Goulasch hongrois

PREPARATION TIME: 25 minutes
COOKING TIME: 1½ hours

INGREDIENTS FOR 4 SERVINGS:
8 ounces (250 g) lean smoked bacon
2 ounces (50 g) butter
2 medium onions, peeled and sliced
1¾ pounds (800 g) blade or chuck steak, cubed
Salt, pepper
2 tablespoons paprika
2 medium tomatoes, peeled and diced
Bouquet garni, made of thyme, bay leaf, and parsley
4 fluid ounces (12 cl) dry white wine
6 tablespoons (10 cl) double cream
2½ pounds (1 kg) potatoes, peeled
Wholemeal bread
Butter

Cut the bacon into ½ inch (1 cm) cubes.

Melt the butter in a large pot or high-sided frying pan, lightly brown the bacon, then add the onions, meat, salt, and pepper. Stir, then sprinkle in the paprika, stir again, and simmer uncovered for 10 to 15 minutes. Add the tomatoes, *bouquet garni*, and wine. Bring just to the boil, then immediately lower the heat, cover the pot, and cook at a very gentle simmer for 1 hour 15 minutes, stirring occasionally (add a little water if necessary so that the meat is always just barely covered by liquid).

Meanwhile, place the potatoes in a large pot, cover with cold water, salt lightly, bring to the boil, and boil gently for 30 minutes. Time it so that the meat and potatoes finish cooking at the same time.

Just before serving, remove the meat from the heat and stir in the cream. Return to the heat just long enough to warm the sauce, but don't allow it to boil. Season with salt and pepper.

Serve, with the potatoes, slices of bread, and a dish of fresh butter all on the side.

STEAK WINE-GROWER'S-STYLE
Entrecôte vigneronne

PREPARATION TIME: 10 minutes
COOKING TIME: about 25 minutes

INGREDIENTS FOR 4 SERVINGS:
1 boneless rib steak weighing 1¾ pounds (800 g)
3 shallots
1 medium onion
2 anchovy fillets in oil
2 ounces (50 g) butter
Salt, pepper
4 fluid ounces (12 cl) red wine

Cut off any excess fat from around the steak.

Finely chop the shallots, onion, and anchovies, either by hand or in a food processor. Place all together in a bowl and reserve for making the sauce.

Melt the butter in a large frying pan until very hot, season the steak with salt and pepper on both sides, then place it in the pan. Cook the steak for 6 minutes on each side over moderately high heat if you like it rare, or 8 minutes on each side if you like it medium rare. When done, lift the meat out of the pan and keep warm while making the sauce.

Stir the chopped onion mixture into the pan and cook for about 5 minutes, or until the onions have softened and begun to brown. Stir in the wine, bring to the boil, and boil for 1 to 2 minutes, or until the sauce has thickened slightly; add salt and pepper if needed.

Either serve the steak as it is on a hot platter and slice it at the table with the sauce in a sauceboat on the side, or slice the meat, strain the sauce, spoon a little on to each dinner plate, place the slices of steak on top, and serve, with any extra sauce in a sauceboat.

VEAL CUTLETS WITH CREAM SAUCE
Côtes de veau

PREPARATION TIME: 15 minutes
COOKING TIME: 15–20 minutes

INGREDIENTS FOR 4 SERVINGS:
2 ounces (60 g) butter
6 medium mushrooms, cleaned and sliced
Salt, pepper
4 veal cutlets weighing about 7 to 8 ounces (200 to 250 g) each
4 fluid ounces (12 cl) dry white wine (preferably Pouilly-Fuissé)
6 tablespoons (10 cl) double cream

Melt a third of the butter in a small frying pan, then add the mushrooms and cook slowly until they soften; season with salt and pepper, and reserve.

In a large frying pan, melt the remaining butter. Season the cutlets with salt and pepper, then place them in the pan, when the butter starts to foam. Cook over moderately high heat for 7 to 8 minutes on each side, then remove from the pan and keep warm while making the sauce.

Pour the wine into the pan the veal was cooked in, stirring over high heat to detach any meat juices stuck to it, then add the mushrooms, cream, and salt and pepper as needed. Heat the sauce to boiling, pour immediately over the veal, and serve.

Serving suggestion: Serve with Spinach (p. 181).

ROAST VEAL WITH OLIVES
Rôti de veau

PREPARATION TIME: 10 minutes
COOKING TIME: 1 hour

INGREDIENTS FOR 4 SERVINGS:
1¾ pounds (800 g) loin of veal
4 ounces (125 g) veal bone or tail, cut into pieces
2 ounces (60 g) butter
1 onion, peeled and sliced
2 medium tomatoes, chopped
Salt
4 ounces (125 g) green olives, stoned

Cut off any large pieces of fat from the veal. In a pot just large enough for the meat, place the scraps of fat, along with the pieces of veal bone or tail, and brown lightly. Add the butter; when it has melted, add the onions and the meat. Cook over moderate heat for 5 to 10 minutes to brown the meat evenly, then add the tomatoes and stir to detach any meat juices stuck to the bottom of the pot. Salt lightly, cover the pot, place over low heat, and simmer for 40 minutes, turning the meat several times as it cooks.

While the meat is cooking, desalt the olives in a bowl of cold water; change the water once or twice.

After the 40 minutes is up, lift the meat out of the pot and place it on a plate. Strain the contents of the pot into a mixing bowl, pressing on the meat and vegetables in the strainer to extract all their juices. Place the strained liquid back in the pot, add the meat, drain the olives, and add them as well, then cover and simmer for 20 minutes longer.

To serve, lift the meat out of the pot and place on a warm platter surrounded by the olives. Serve the sauce in a sauceboat on the side.

Serving suggestion: Serve with Mashed Potatoes (p. 204).

FAMILY-STYLE BRAISED BEEF
Bœuf mode

PREPARATION TIME: 20 minutes
COOKING TIME: 3 hours

INGREDIENTS FOR 4 SERVINGS:
2¼ pounds (1 kg) sirloin or silverside of beef
About 4 ounces (125 g) rindless back pork fat (for larding)
½ calf's foot
Salt, pepper
8 ounces (250 g) bacon, diced
6 small onions, peeled
6 carrots, peeled, halved lengthwise, and quartered
Bouquet garni, made of thyme, bay leaf, and parsley
18 fluid ounces (50 cl) dry white wine
7 fluid ounces (20 cl) water

Lard the beef with strips of pork fat, using a larding needle (or ask your butcher to do it). Season the meat and calf's foot with salt and pepper.

In a large stew pot, melt the butter. When it starts to foam, add the onions and bacon, and brown over high heat, stirring frequently. Add the beef and calf's foot, brown on all sides, then add the carrots, *bouquet garni*, and wine. Simmer uncovered for 1 hour, during which time some of the wine should evaporate. Add the water, salt, and pepper. Turn the meat over, bring to the boil, then cover the pot and simmer slowly for 2 hours (this dish must cook very slowly and for a long time).

To serve, discard the *bouquet garni*, then lift the meat and calf's foot out of the pot. Carve the meat and cut the foot into pieces, then place them on a hot platter, surrounded by the vegetables and bacon. Use a spoon to skim off the fat on the surface of the cooking liquid, then pour the liquid over the meat and serve.

Serving suggestions: Serve with Mashed Potatoes (p. 204), Split Pea Purée (p. 197), or Rice Pilaf (p. 224).

VARIATION: Leftovers are delicious eaten cold; as a matter of fact, some people always eat this dish cold rather than hot. Place the meat in a deep dish or bowl, arrange the carrots and onions around it and on top of it, then strain the cooking liquid over it. Leave to cool, then refrigerate overnight before serving. Serve with a Green Salad (p. 66) (see photo).

Family-style Braised Beef

VEAL BIRDS AND OLIVES
Oiseaux sans tête

PREPARATION TIME: 30 minutes
COOKING TIME: about 35 minutes

INGREDIENTS FOR 4 SERVINGS:
4 ounces (125 g) green olives, stoned
8 thin veal escalopes weighing about 2½ to 3 ounces (70 to 80 g) each
Salt, pepper
8 thin slices ham
4 tablespoons olive oil
2 onions, peeled and chopped
8 ounces (250 g) tomatoes, peeled and chopped
Bouquet garni, made of thyme, bay leaf, and parsley
1 clove garlic, whole and unpeeled

Soak the olives in lukewarm water for 30 minutes.

In the meantime, make the veal birds: place the veal escalopes on the table, and season with salt and pepper. Place a piece of ham (it should be about the same size as the escalope) on top of each one, fold in the ends, then roll each one up like a sausage. Tie with kitchen string, with one piece going around the "bird" lengthwise and the other crosswise, like a little package.

Heat the oil in a large frying pan, add the onions, and cook to colour lightly; then add the veal birds and brown on all sides over moderate heat. Add the tomatoes, the *bouquet garni*, and the garlic. Raise the heat and boil for about 10 minutes, or until the water from the vegetables has all evaporated; then lower the heat, cover the pan, and cook for 8 minutes. Add the olives and cook for 7 minutes more, taste for salt and pepper, and serve.

Serving suggestions: these are delicious with Mashed Potatoes (p. 204) or Potato Soufflé (p. 206).

Veal birds are also very good cold, served with a Green Salad (p. 66).

VEAL BLANQUETTE
Blanquette de veau

PREPARATION TIME: 20 minutes
COOKING TIME: 1½ hours

INGREDIENTS FOR 4 SERVINGS:
2 pounds (1 kg) breast of veal or pie
    veal
1¼ pint (75 cl) water
Bouquet garni, made with 2 celery
    stalks, 1 sprig thyme, and ¼ bay
    leaf tied together
3 carrots, peeled and cut into thick
    sticks
12 baby onions, peeled

3 peppercorns
1 teaspoon coarse salt
2 ounces (60 g) butter
1 ounce (30 g) flour
2 egg yolks
6 tablespoons (10 cl) double cream
1 tablespoon lemon juice
Pepper
1 tablespoon chopped parsley

Cut the veal into pieces about the size of an egg. Place in a pot, add the water (the meat should be almost, but not quite, covered), and bring to the boil, skimming off any foam that rises. Add the *bouquet garni*, along with the carrots, onions, peppercorns, and salt as soon as the water comes to the boil. Cover the pot, lower the heat, and simmer slowly for 1 hour.

Lift the meat and vegetables out of the pot with a slotted spoon, place in a serving dish, and keep warm while making the sauce. Discard the *bouquet garni*.

In a saucepan, melt the butter, then stir in the flour. When the mixture is smooth (do not allow to colour), add the cooking liquid from the veal, little by little, whisking constantly. Once all the liquid has been added, bring to the boil and boil rapidly for 2 to 3 minutes to thicken the sauce, then remove the pot from the heat.

In a mixing bowl, whisk together the egg yolks and cream. Ladle in a little of the hot sauce, whisking constantly. Add the lemon juice, then pour back into the pot stirring constantly. The sauce should be very hot but not boiling. Add a little pepper, pour the sauce over the meat and vegetables, sprinkle with parsley, and serve immediately.

VEAL WITH BABY VEGETABLES
Jarret de veau primeurs

PREPARATION TIME: 20 minutes
COOKING TIME: 1½ hours

INGREDIENTS FOR 4 SERVINGS:
1 shin of veal, weighing about 2¾
    pounds (1.25 kg)
Salt, pepper
3 ounces (90 g) butter
2 cloves garlic, whole and unpeeled
3 tomatoes, peeled and chopped
1 tablespoon olive oil
8 ounces (250 g) new
    carrots, peeled and cut in half
    lengthwise (larger carrots should be
    halved lengthwise and quartered)
1 pound (500 g) new potatoes, peeled
    and cut in half lengthwise

Season the meat with salt and pepper before cooking.

Over moderate heat, melt two-thirds of the butter in a pot just large enough to hold the veal. When hot, add the veal and a clove of garlic, and brown for about 15 minutes, turning frequently. Add the tomatoes, cover the pot, lower the heat, and simmer for 1½ hours, turning the meat occasionally. If the liquid from the tomatoes evaporates and the meat begins to stick, add a little warm water to the pot.

While the meat finishes cooking, heat the remaining butter and the oil in a large frying pan. Add the carrots and potatoes (they should all fit on the bottom of the pan, or almost), garlic, salt, and pepper. Cook the vegetables until lightly browned, then lower the heat and cook very slowly for 15 to 20 minutes or until done, shaking the pan frequently.

Lift the veal out of the pot and carve it on a board. Season with salt and pepper. Place on a hot platter, surrounded with the vegetables. Taste the cooking liquid for salt and pepper, and serve in a sauceboat on the side.

Serving suggestion: Serve with a Green Salad (p. 66).

Note: Two or three whole tomatoes, peeled, placed in a roasting pan, seasoned with salt, pepper, and a few spoonfuls of olive oil, can be roasted in a hot oven for about 20 minutes and served as well (see photo). Ed.

Veal with Baby Vegetables

LEG OF LAMB ENGLISH-STYLE
Gigot à l'anglaise

PREPARATION TIME: 10 minutes
COOKING TIME: 20 minutes per pound

INGREDIENTS FOR 5 TO 6 SERVINGS:
6 pints (3½ litres) water
1 ounce (30 g) coarse salt
2 onions, peeled and quartered
2 carrots, peeled and sliced
4 sprigs parsley
1 sprig thyme
1 bay leaf
2 celery stalks
3 peppercorns
3½ pounds (1.6 kg) leg of lamb, excess fat removed

Bring the water to the boil in a pot large enough to hold the lamb comfortably. Add the salt, onions, carrots, parsley, thyme, bay leaf, celery, and peppercorns. When the liquid is boiling rapidly, add the lamb and cook for 20 minutes per pound at a very slow, even boil. Skim off any foam that rises. When the cooking time is up, remove the pot from the heat, but leave the lamb in the liquid for an additional 20 minutes. Lift it out and carve into thick slices. Sprinkle with salt and pepper, place on a hot platter, and serve.

Serving suggestions: Serve with Baked Potatoes with Tomatoes (p. 202) and a Green Salad (p. 66). Any leftovers are delicious served cold with pickled gherkins and mustard.

Note: This plain dish can be livened up, if you like, with a Garlic Mayonnaise (p. 84) or Gribiche Sauce (p. 86) served in a sauceboat on the side. Ed.

ROAST SHOULDER OF LAMB
Epaule d'agneau à la broche

PREPARATION TIME: 10 minutes
COOKING TIME: 15 minutes per pound

INGREDIENTS FOR 6 SERVINGS:
2 cloves garlic
A 2¾-pound (1.25-kg) boned shoulder of lamb (weight without bone)
Salt, pepper
4 fluid ounces (12 cl) water (for the roasting pan)
6 tablespoons (10 cl) water (for the sauce)
1 ounce (30 g) softened butter, cut into 5 pieces

Peel the garlic and cut each clove into three wedges. Use a small knife to make six incisions in the meat and slide a wedge of garlic into each one. Season the meat generously with salt and pepper. Roll and tie into a sausage-like shape if the butcher hasn't already done so.

Roast the lamb on a spit if possible (see *Note*). Preheat for about 15 minutes, then spit the lamb, set it into place, pour 4 fluid ounces (12 cl) of warm water into the drippings pan under the meat, and roast for 20 minutes per pound. Turn off the heat and leave the lamb turning on the spit for 5 to 7 minutes more before making the sauce and serving (the meat will be very rare, as it should be).

To serve, remove the meat from the spit, place on a board, and carve, being careful not to lose any of the juices that come out of the meat. Place the meat on a warm platter. Add the meat juices as well as 6 tablespoons of water to the roasting pan and bring to the boil, scraping the bottom of the pan to dissolve anything stuck to it. Stir in the butter, season with salt and pepper lightly, then pour the sauce into a sauceboat to serve on the side.

Serve immediately.

Serving suggestions: Serve with Haricot Beans Provençale (p. 193) or French Beans (p. 192).

Note: If you don't have a rotisserie, cook the lamb in the oven. Preheat the oven to 425°F (220°C or Mark 7), place the lamb in a roasting pan, and roast for 15 minutes per pound. Turn off the oven but leave the lamb inside for 7 minutes, then carve and make the sauce as described above, but in this case, add 4 fluid ounces (12 cl) water to the roasting pan before adding the butter. Ed.

133

LAMB STEW
Sauté d'agneau

PREPARATION TIME: 20 minutes
COOKING TIME: 50 minutes

INGREDIENTS FOR 4 SERVINGS:
1 pound (500 g) neck of lamb, cut into 5 or 6 pieces
1¼ pounds (600 g) shoulder of lamb, cut into 5 or 6 pieces
Salt, pepper
3 ounces (80 g) butter
4 carrots, peeled and cut into thick sticks
12 baby onions, peeled
Bouquet garni, made with 2 celery stalks, 1 sprig thyme, and ¼ bay leaf tied
    together
1 tablespoon flour
4 fluid ounces (12 cl) dry white wine
3 medium tomatoes, peeled and chopped
1 pound (500 g) new potatoes, peeled

Generously season the lamb with salt and pepper.

Melt the butter in a large, high-sided frying pan or stew pot. When it starts to foam, add the meat and cook over high heat until brown, turning frequently. Add the carrots, onions, and *bouquet garni*, cook for 5 to 10 minutes to brown the vegetables, then stir in the flour, the wine, and the tomatoes. Bring to the boil, stirring constantly, then immediately lower the heat, cover the pot, and simmer for 10 minutes. Add the potatoes, cover, and cook for 30 minutes more, stirring from time to time. Season with salt and pepper when the potatoes are done.

Serve immediately, either in the cooking pot or in a serving dish.

Serving suggestion: Serve with a Green Salad (p. 66) on the side.

ROAST PORK WITH MUSTARD
Rôti de porc à la moutarde

PREPARATION TIME: 20 minutes
COOKING TIME: about 1½ hours

INGREDIENTS FOR 4 SERVINGS:
3½ ounces (100 g) Dijon mustard
2 pounds (900 g) loin or fillet of pork
About 6 ounces (175 g) pig's caul or thin rashers of fatty bacon
8 baby onions, peeled
Salt, pepper
4 fluid ounces (12 cl) dry white wine
4 tablespoons hot water

Preheat the oven to 425°F (220°C or Mark 7).

Use a small spoon to spread the mustard all over the pork, then spread out the caul and completely wrap the pork up in it (if using slices of bacon, tie them around the joint from end to end). Tie off both ends of the caul, then tie two strings around the joint to hold the fat in place.

Place the meat in a roasting pan, surround with the onions, season with salt and pepper, add the wine, and place in the oven. Once the roast begins to brown, baste it every 10 or 15 minutes. Cook for a total of 1 hour 20 minutes, then turn off the oven but leave the roast inside for an additional 10 minutes.

Lift the roast out and place on a warm serving platter; place the roasting pan on top of the stove and boil the pan juices over high heat, add the hot water and a little pepper, boil rapidly for about 10 seconds, then pour into a sauceboat and serve with the meat.

Serving suggestions: Serve with Potatoes au Gratin (p. 209) or Split Pea Purée (p. 197). Roast pork is also excellent cold with a green salad, so don't be afraid of making too much (if using a larger roast, remember to increase the cooking time proportionally).

BOILED PORK DINNER
Potée au chou

PREPARATION TIME: 20 minutes (plus time to desalt)
COOKING TIME: 1¾ hours

INGREDIENTS FOR 4 TO 6 SERVINGS:
8 ounces (250 g) salt belly pork
1 salted shoulder of pork weighing about 2¼ pounds (1 kg)
8 ounces (250 g) salt pork rind
7 pints (4 litres) cold water (for the meat)
1 onion, peeled and stuck with a clove
Bouquet garni, made with 1 sprig thyme and 1 bay leaf tied together
4 peppercorns
1 small green cabbage
3½ pints (2 litres) water (for the cabbage)
4 celery stalks
4 leeks, cleaned and split lengthwise
4 turnips, peeled
1 pound (500 g) small potatoes

Salt pork must be desalted before cooking, generally 6 hours to overnight. Place it in a large bowl or pot, cover with cold water, and leave for the required time, changing the water at least two or three times (when you buy the pork, ask how long to desalt it).

Place the pork (belly, shoulder, and rind) in a large pot, add 7 pints (4 litres) cold water, the onion, *bouquet garni*, and peppercorns. Bring the water to the boil, skimming off any foam, then lower the heat and simmer for 1 hour 15 minutes.

While the pork is cooking, prepare the vegetables. Cut the cabbage into 4 pieces. Bring 3½ pints (2 litres) of unsalted water to the boil in a large pot, add the cabbage, and boil for 10 minutes, then drain in a colander. Tie the celery and leeks together with kitchen string, and peel the turnips and potatoes.

Add the vegetables to the pot with the pork, cover, and cook for 30 minutes more.

To serve, lift the vegetables out with a slotted spoon and place them on a hot platter. Lift out the pork, carve it on a board and place it on the platter with the vegetables. Serve with variously flavoured mustards, black olives, and wholemeal bread on the side.

SAUSAGES WITH WHITE WINE
Saucisses au vin blanc

PREPARATION TIME: 10 minutes
COOKING TIME: 20 minutes

INGREDIENTS FOR 4 SERVINGS:
8 pure pork sausages
1½ ounces (40 g) butter
1 onion, peeled and finely chopped
1 clove garlic, peeled and finely chopped
4 fluid ounces (12 cl) dry white wine
Salt, pepper

Prick the sausages in several places to keep them from bursting open while cooking.

Melt the butter in a frying pan. When hot, add the sausages and onion, and brown over moderate heat for about 10 minutes. Add the garlic and wine, stirring to detach any juices stuck to the bottom of the pan. Cook for 5 to 8 minutes more, then lift the sausages out of the pan and keep warm on a platter.

Add a little warm water to the cooking liquids in the pan if there isn't enough left to make a light sauce. Bring to the boil, season with freshly ground pepper and a little salt, stir, then pour over the sausages and serve.

Serving suggestions: Serve with Mashed Potatoes (p. 204) or Split Pea Purée (p. 197).

SAUERKRAUT WITH SALT PORK
Choucroûte fraîche

PREPARATION TIME: 40 minutes (plus desalting the pork)
COOKING TIME: 1½–2 hours

INGREDIENTS FOR 6 TO 8 SERVINGS:
2¾ pounds (1.25 kg) fresh, raw sauerkraut
1 lightly salted shoulder of pork, weighing about 2¼ pounds (1 kg)
8 ounces (250 g) lightly salted belly pork
About 5 ounces (150 g) salt pork rind
1 clove garlic, peeled
5 juniper berries
5 peppercorns
1 teaspoon caraway seeds
2 sprigs thyme
¼ bay leaf
3½ ounces (100 g) goose fat or lard
2 carrots, peeled and sliced
2 onions, peeled and sliced
18 fluid ounces (50 cl) dry white wine (preferably from Alsace)
12 ounces (350 g) pure pork poaching sausage
6 to 8 pure pork frankfurters
6 to 8 small new potatoes, peeled
Dijon mustard (for serving)

Buy only fresh, raw (uncooked) sauerkraut; the whiter it is the better.

Soak all the salt pork (shoulder, belly, and rind) to desalt, in a large pot or bowl of cold water for 1½ hours if it is very lightly salted, otherwise overnight – ask how long to soak it when you purchase it.

Place the sauerkraut in a colander and rinse it under cold running water, lifting and spreading it out to wash it thoroughly; then drain it and squeeze out all the water with your hands.

Tie the garlic, juniper berries, peppercorns, caraway, thyme, and bay leaf inside a little piece of thin cloth and reserve.

Melt half the goose fat or lard in a large pot, add the carrots and onions, cook to colour lightly, then pour in the wine and add the sauerkraut. It should be barely covered with liquid to cook properly, so add water to the pot if necessary. Spread the remaining goose fat or lard over the surface, bring just to the boil, then immediately lower the heat, cover the pot, and cook over very low heat for 1½ to 2 hours, stirring from time to time.

Meanwhile, cook the meat separately. Place the rind, fat side down,

(Continued p. 140)

Sauerkraut with Salt Pork

in the bottom of a large pot, then add the shoulder, belly, the little bag of spices, and enough water or bouillon to cover by about 2 inches (5 cm). Bring to the boil, then lower the heat and simmer slowly for 1½ to 2 hours. Thirty minutes before the meat has finished cooking, add the sausages and potatoes to it.

To serve, place the sauerkraut in the centre of a large, hot platter and surround it with the meat, rind, sausages, and potatoes. Serve accompanied by several different mustards.

BOUDIN WITH ONIONS
Boudin noir

PREPARATION TIME: 30 minutes

INGREDIENTS FOR 4 SERVINGS:
1 pound (500 g) *boudin* (see *Note*)
1 ounce (30 g) butter
2 onions, peeled and sliced
Salt, pepper

Cut the *boudin* into pieces about 6 inches (15 cm) long, then prick each one in several places with a pin so they won't burst open while cooking. Heat the butter in a frying pan until it starts to foam, then add the onions and brown over moderate heat for 10 to 15 minutes. Remove them from the pan with a slotted spoon and keep warm while cooking the *boudin*.

Place the *boudin* in the same pan and cook over moderate heat for 15 minutes, turning frequently. Season with a little salt and pepper.

Place the onions on a hot platter, place the pieces of *boudin* on top, and serve immediately.

Serving suggestion: Serve with Mashed Potatoes (p. 204).

Note: Boudin is a French black pudding (blood sausage); although not quite the same, blutwurst, when available, could be used instead. Ed.

7

POULTRY AND GAME

Whenever possible, buy fresh rather than frozen poultry; the difference in taste is enormous.

A *boiling fowl* is a female chicken that is no longer used for laying eggs. The best generally weigh 3½ to 5 pounds (1.6 to 2.25 kg).

A *roaster* is a tender young chicken, weighing from 2½ to 5 pounds (1.15 to 2.25 kg).

A *capon*, a castrated male chicken specially raised and fattened to produce very tender flesh, weighs from 5 to 8 pounds (2.25 to 3.6 kg).

A *cock* or *rooster*, an adult male chicken, lean and tough, used generally in stews, weighs from 8¾ to 11 pounds (4 to 5 kg).

When buying *turkey*, choose birds with well-developed breast meat (the breast bone should not form a ridge) and fine white skin.

Pigeon: choose young birds (squab) with large feet and pink flesh on the wings, weighing no more than 1 pound (450 g).

When buying *duck*, choose young ones weighing 3 to 5½ pounds (1.4 to 2.5 kg) with tight white skin and plump breasts.

When buying *rabbit*, look for young animals weighing 2 to 3½ pounds (900 g to 1.6 kg), with meaty thighs and white fat.

Guinea hen, although domesticated, is somewhat similar to pheasant. It should have yellow skin and meaty breasts with pale reddish flesh.

Young *pheasants* can be recognized by the small size of the spur on the underside of the foot. Females are generally preferred to the more spectacularly feathered males.

DUCK WITH TURNIPS
Canard aux navets

PREPARATION TIME: 35 minutes
COOKING TIME: about 50 minutes

INGREDIENTS FOR 4 SERVINGS:

A 3-pound (1.4-kg) duck with liver, heart, and lungs
4 ounces (125 g) lean bacon, diced
2 large shallots, peeled and chopped (for stuffing)
3 duck or chicken livers, chopped to a paste (for stuffing)
1 pinch powdered thyme

1 pinch powdered bay leaf
2 tablespoons chopped parsley
1½ ounces (40 g) coarsely crumbled dry or stale toast (or melba toast)
2 egg yolks
1 pinch 4-spice mixture (see *Note*) or allspice

(Continued p. 142)

2 pounds (900 g) turnips (see *Note*)
Butter (for 2 roasting pans)
7 fluid ounces (20 cl) double cream
Salt, pepper
Nutmeg

1 shallot, peeled and finely chopped
(for the sauce)
1 tablespoon brandy
1 ounce (25 g) softened butter, cut
into 5 pieces

The duck should be cleaned and prepared for roasting; save the heart, liver, and lungs for the sauce. If you remove the wishbone, which is right where the two breasts meet in the front, the duck will be easier to carve.

Preheat the oven to 425°F (220°C or Mark 7).

Mix together the diced bacon, shallots, the duck or chicken livers for the stuffing, thyme, bay leaf, parsley, crumbled toast, and egg yolks. Season with the 4-spice mixture, then stuff the duck and carefully sew it closed so the stuffing will stay inside.

When the duck is ready to roast, prepare the turnips. Peel and slice them as thinly as possible, drop them into lightly salted boiling water, bring back to the boil, and boil 2 minutes; then drain. Lightly butter a baking dish just large enough to hold the turnips and place them so that the slices slightly overlap; when half of them are in the dish, season with salt, pepper, and nutmeg, then finish filling the dish, spoon over the cream, and season once more with salt, pepper, and nutmeg. Reserve.

Place the duck in a lightly buttered roasting pan, add 4 tablespoons of water, and roast for a total of 50 minutes or until the breast is tender. After 20 minutes, place the turnips in the oven as well, and continue cooking for the final 30 minutes.

Chop the duck's liver, heart, and lungs to a paste. Mix with the shallot, place in a small saucepan with the brandy, season with a little salt and pepper, and cook over very low heat for 1 minute; remove from the heat.

When the duck is done, remove it from the oven but do not switch off the heat. Carve the duck on a board, being careful to save any juices that come from it. First remove the legs and thighs and place them on a piece of aluminium foil, skin side down; put them back in the oven to continue cooking while you finish carving the duck and make the sauce.

Place the sliced duck breasts on a hot platter with the stuffing and keep warm. Discard almost all the fat in the roasting pan. Add the carving juices, the brandy-liver mixture, 5 tablespoons warm water, and the softened butter and heat on top of the stove, stirring, until the butter has melted. Pour into a sauceboat. Remove the legs from the oven, place on the serving platter, and serve, with the turnips and sauce on the side.

Note: The French 4-spice mixture (quatre épices) *is a commercial mixture that varies in strength. You can make one version using 10 parts ground pepper, 5 parts ground nutmeg, 3 parts ground cloves, and 2 parts ground ginger.*

The turnip in the photo is a black variety preferred by Paul Bocuse for its delicate taste. Ed.

Duck with Turnips

BOILED CHICKEN
Poule bouillie

PREPARATION TIME: 25 minutes
COOKING TIME: 1½ hours

INGREDIENTS FOR 6 SERVINGS:
A 4-pound (1.8-kg) boiling fowl
4 small leeks, cleaned
½ head celery, split lengthwise
Bouquet garni, made of 1 sprig thyme, ¼ bay leaf, and 4 sprigs parsley tied
   together
6 medium carrots, peeled and cut in half lengthwise
2 onions, peeled (one stuck with a clove)
3 small turnips, peeled and cut in half
1 tomato, peeled
4 teaspoons (30 g) coarse salt
3 peppercorns
6 medium potatoes, peeled

Cut the wing tips and neck off the hen and chop into small pieces; tie the bird as for roasting, and place with the neck and wings in a large pot.

Tie the leeks and celery together with kitchen string. Add these, along with the *bouquet garni*, carrots, onions, turnips, and tomato to the pot. Pour in enough cold water to cover completely. Add the salt and peppercorns, then bring to the boil, immediately lower the heat, skim off any foam, and cover the pot. Simmer for 1 hour. Add the potatoes and cook for 30 minutes more.

To serve, ladle out and strain enough of the bouillon to serve first as a soup, with slices of toasted brown bread (save any leftover bouillon for use in other recipes). Remove and discard the *bouquet garni*, then lift the chicken out of the pot and carve. Place on a hot platter, surround with the vegetables, and serve, with various Dijon mustards (flavoured and unflavoured), a bowl of coarse salt (to sprinkle over the meat), and pickled gherkins on the side.

STUFFED BOILED CHICKEN
Poularde farcie

PREPARATION TIME: 25 minutes
COOKING TIME: 2 hours

INGREDIENTS FOR 4 TO 6 SERVINGS:

A 3½-pound (1.6-kg) boiling fowl
4 chicken livers, chopped
2 ounces (50 g) fresh breadcrumbs
4 fluid ounces (12 cl) milk
2 shallots, peeled and finely chopped
1 large clove garlic, peeled and
  finely chopped
2 tablespoons finely chopped parsley
3½ ounces (100 g) lean bacon, chopped
1 egg
Salt, pepper

1 sprig thyme
¼ bay leaf
4 peppercorns
1 onion, peeled and stuck with a clove
About 6 pints (3½ litres) water
1 tablespoon coarse salt
4 to 6 large leeks, cleaned and tied
  together
4 to 6 medium carrots, peeled
2 to 3 celery stalks, strings removed

First make the stuffing. Chop the bird's liver and heart, and reserve in a bowl with the other chopped livers. Place the crumbled bread in another bowl with the milk and leave for about 10 minutes, or until the bread has completely softened. Use the prongs of a fork to crush the bread, then stir in the livers, shallots, garlic, parsley, bacon, and egg. Season generously with salt and pepper, then stuff the hen and sew it up so that none of the stuffing will escape while cooking.

Place the bird in a large pot with the thyme, bay leaf, peppercorns, and onion. Pour in enough water to cover completely, add the salt, and bring to the boil. Skim off any foam, then lower the heat, cover the pot and simmer for 1 hour. Add the leeks, carrots, and celery, and cook for 1 hour more.

Remove the bird from the pot, carve it, and serve on a hot platter with the stuffing and vegetables around it, and mustard and pickled gherkins on the side.

If you like, the cooking liquid (bouillon) can be served first, as a soup, with slices of toasted brown bread. (Any leftover bouillon can be used for other recipes.)

POT-ROASTED CHICKEN
Poulet cocotte

PREPARATION TIME: 30 minutes
COOKING TIME: 40 minutes

INGREDIENTS FOR 4 TO 5 SERVINGS:
4 rashers lean bacon
A 3-pound (1.4-kg) chicken (reserve the liver and gizzard)
2 ounces (60 g) butter
Salt, pepper
2¼ pounds (1 kg) new potatoes, peeled (cut larger potatoes in half)
1 tablespoon olive oil
16 baby onions, peeled
¼ teaspoon dried thyme
4 tablespoons boiling water.

Cover the breasts and thighs of the chicken with the bacon, and tie the slices in place with string or attach them with toothpicks.

Melt half the butter in a pot slightly larger than the chicken, add the chicken along with its liver and gizzard, and cook over low heat, turning frequently for even browning, for 20 minutes. Season with salt and pepper.

Peel the potatoes, wash in cold water, then drain and pat dry with a cloth.

While the chicken is browning, heat the remaining butter and the oil in a frying pan. Add the onions, potatoes, and thyme. Cook for 20 minutes, shaking the pan to brown the vegetables evenly. Season with salt and pepper. When the cooking time is up, lift the vegetables out of the pan with a slotted spoon, add them to the pot with the chicken, cover, and continue cooking over a low heat for 15 minutes.

To serve, lift the chicken out of the pot and carve. Place on a hot platter and surround with the vegetables. Pour the boiling water into the pot the chicken was cooked in, bring to the boil, stirring constantly, season with salt and pepper if needed, and serve in a sauceboat on the side.

Serving suggestion: Serve with one of the salads (pp. 65–8)

CHICKEN IN CREAM SAUCE LOUHANS-STYLE

Poulet de Bresse sauté à la crème comme à Louhans

PREPARATION TIME: 30 minutes
COOKING TIME: 40 minutes

INGREDIENTS FOR 4 TO 5 SERVINGS:
A 3-pound (1.4-kg) roasting chicken
Salt, pepper
2 ounces (60 g) butter
8 baby onions, peeled
3 cloves garlic, whole and unpeeled
1 carrot, peeled and sliced
1 tablespoon flour
½ bottle dry white wine (preferably a Mâcon)
1 pint (50 cl) water
Bouquet garni, made of thyme, bay leaf, and parsley tied together
6 fluid ounces (20 cl) double cream; *or* egg yolks, 6 tablespoons (10 cl) double
   cream, and 1 tablespoon lemon juice
Salt, pepper

Cut the chicken into 8 pieces (wings and breasts separated, thighs and drumsticks separated), then chop the back and carcass into several pieces as well. Season with salt and pepper.

Melt the butter in a high-sided frying pan just large enough to hold all the pieces of chicken on the bottom. First brown the breast meat and wings; lift them out and brown the thighs and drumsticks with the onions, garlic, and carrots; lift them out and brown the back and carcass (leave the vegetables in the pan). When the back has browned, return the other pieces of chicken to the pan, sprinkle in the flour, stirring and turning over the pieces of chicken, then add the wine, water, and *bouquet garni*. Bring to the boil, stirring, and cook over high heat for 20 minutes, or until ⅔ of the liquid has evaporated. Lift out the onions and the chicken, except the pieces of back and carcass, and keep warm while finishing the sauce. Boil the remaining liquid over high heat to evaporate by half.

The sauce can be finished in one of two ways. In either case, strain it first into a clean saucepan. Then either simply add 6 fluid ounces (20 cl) of cream and cook for about 4 minutes, or until thick and creamy. Or, thicken the sauce with egg yolks and cream. In this case, whisk the egg yolks and 6 tablespoons of cream together in a mixing bowl, add a small ladleful of the strained sauce, whisking rapidly, then pour the mixture into the saucepan, whisking constantly. Heat over low heat until very

147

hot, but do not allow to boil; then add the lemon juice, and taste for salt and pepper. The chicken and onions can be reheated in the sauce if need be, but stir the sauce constantly in this case and do not allow it to boil or it will curdle.

When the sauce is ready, spoon it over the chicken and onions on a hot platter and serve.

Serving suggestion: Serve with Spinach (p. 181).

COCK IN RED WINE
Coq au vin de Juliénas

PREPARATION TIME: 30 minutes
COOKING TIME: about 1 to 1½ hours

INGREDIENTS FOR 6 SERVINGS:
A 4¾ to 6½ pound (2.2 to 3 kg) cock bird or boiling fowl (see *Note*)
Blood from the bird (see *Note*)
2 cloves garlic
1½ ounces (40 g) butter
5 ounces (150 g) bacon, cut into cubes
8 baby onions, peeled
1 large tomato, peeled and quartered
1 medium carrot, peeled and quartered
Bouquet garni made with 2 sprigs thyme, ¼ bay leaf, 4 sprigs parsley, 1 celery
  stalk and the white of 1 leek, tied together
8 medium mushrooms, whole and unpeeled
1 generous tablespoon flour
3 tablespoons cognac
1½ bottles red wine (preferably Juliénas)
Salt, pepper

If possible, order a freshly killed bird and ask that its blood be saved for making the sauce (see *Note*).

Clean the bird and reserve the liver, heart and lungs. Cut off the legs and separate the thighs from the drumsticks, cut off the breasts and divide them in half at the wing, then chop the remaining carcass, neck, and back into several large pieces. Sprinkle with salt and reserve.

Chop the liver, heart and lungs to a paste and add to the blood, along with 1 garlic clove, peeled and chopped.

Melt the butter in a large pot, add the chicken, bacon, and onions and brown turning frequently for about 7 minutes. Add the tomato, carrot, mushrooms, *bouquet garni* and remaining garlic clove, whole and unpeeled. Cook slowly, uncovered, for 7 minutes more, then sprinkle in the flour and stir to combine. Cook for 5 minutes, pour in the cognac and boil for a few seconds, stirring to dissolve the juices stuck to the bottom of the pan. Add the wine, bring just to the boil, then immediately lower the heat and cook at a slow boil, uncovered, for 1 to 1½ hours. Test to see if the chicken is done by piercing a drumstick with the tip of a knife or skewer – if it goes in easily the bird is cooked.

Remove the pieces of chicken from the pan; discard the pieces of back and carcass which were just to flavour the sauce. Remove the onions, bacon, and mushrooms with a slotted spoon and reserve.

Strain the remaining sauce, return to the pot and boil for 5 to 10

149

minutes, then remove from the heat and stir in the liver mixture. Place over low heat and heat just until the sauce thickens; do not allow to boil. Place the chicken, bacon, onions and mushrooms back in the pot to warm through, taste for salt and pepper, then serve in the pot it was cooked in.

Note: The blood used to flavour and thicken the sauce need not necessarily come from the bird in question. 6 tablespoons of pig's blood may be used instead, but if neither is available, 5 chicken livers (including the one from the chicken you are using) may be used. Sauté them for 1 to 2 minutes in a little butter or oil over high heat, then drain on paper towels and allow to cool. Place in a blender or food processor with 5 fluid ounces (15 cl) of the sauce and blend until smooth, then whisk this mixture into the sauce. If you would like the sauce to be thicker, add a little beurre manié *as described in the recipe for Hare Stewed in Red Wine, p. 161, using the measurements given there.*

A true cock is a much larger bird than the one used here, weighing from 8¾ to 11 pounds (4 to 5 kg) with tough, but very tasty flesh, not unlike the dark meat on a turkey. It is large enough to feed 8 to 10 people. If you make this recipe with a cock, double all the measurements and the cooking time, and brown the bird in batches. Otherwise follow the recipe exactly as described. Ed.

CHICKEN LIVER SOUFFLÉ
Gâteau aux foies de volaille

PREPARATION TIME: 30 minutes
COOKING TIME: 40 minutes and 45 minutes

INGREDIENTS FOR 4 SERVINGS:
2¼ pounds (1 kg) fresh tomatoes
4 teaspoons olive oil
Bouquet garni, made with 1 sprig thyme,
  ¼ bay leaf and 1 celery stalk tied together
1 teaspoon granulated sugar
Salt, pepper
3 chicken livers, about 4 ounces (125 g),
  finely chopped (see *Note*)

1 small onion, peeled and sliced
Milk (for the onion)
3½ ounces (100 g) stale bread, crumbled
1 pint (50 cl) milk (for the bread)
1 clove garlic, peeled and finely chopped
2 tablespoons chopped parsley
4 eggs, separated
1 ounce (20 g) butter (for the soufflé dish)

Fresh tomato sauce is always excellent – this one is a little different from the one in the chapter on Sauces.

Peel the tomatoes, cut them into wedges, and place in a saucepan with 1 teaspoon of the olive oil and the *bouquet garni*. Add the sugar, bring to the boil, then lower the heat and boil gently over moderate heat for about 40 minutes or until thick, stirring frequently. Season with salt and pepper. Just before serving remove the *bouquet garni* and stir in the remaining olive oil.

Preheat the oven to 350°F (180°C or Mark 4).

While the sauce is cooking you can make the soufflé. If possible buy livers that are light in colour – they are the best. So that the onion will be more digestible, place the slices in a saucepan, add enough cold milk to cover, bring just to a boil, then drain and reserve.

Place the bread in a bowl, add the milk; once the bread has softened, crush it with the prongs of a fork, then pour off any excess milk. Place the bread on a cutting board with the livers, onion, garlic and parsley, and chop to a paste. Place in a mixing bowl, stir in the egg yolks, and season with salt and pepper.

Place the butter in a 7-inch (18-cm) soufflé dish and place it in the oven just long enough for the butter to melt. Remove from the oven and turn the dish to coat the sides with the butter.

Beat the egg whites until stiff and fold them into the liver mixture, then pour into the soufflé dish. Place in the oven and bake for 45 minutes (check for browning by looking through the window in the oven door if possible, but don't open it until the soufflé is done). Serve the soufflé immediately it comes from the oven, with the tomato sauce in a sauceboat on the side.

Note: This recipe, which is made in many homes around Lyons, was devised to use leftover chicken livers so they don't go to waste. It can be made with as few as 1 liver, or as many as 6, so if you like chicken livers, don't hesitate to double the measurement given in the list of ingredients.

BOILED MIXED MEAT AND TURKEY DINNER
Dindonne au pot

PREPARATION TIME: 20 minutes
COOKING TIME: 1½ hours

INGREDIENTS FOR 6 TO 8 SERVINGS:
About 7 pints (4 litres) cold water
Bouquet garni, made of 1 leek, 2 celery stalks, 1 sprig thyme, and ¼ bay leaf
   tied together
2 onions, peeled and stuck with 1 clove each
4 carrots, peeled and quartered
1 rounded tablespoon coarse salt
4 peppercorns
A 4½ pound (2 kg) oven-ready turkey (see *Note*)
1 oxtail, cut into pieces
1 veal knuckle
6 fluid ounces (18 cl) walnut or other salad oil
3 tablespoons red wine vinegar
Salt, pepper
2 tablespoons finely chopped chervil

Fill a very large pot with the cold water, add the *bouquet garni*, onions, carrots, salt and peppercorns; then add all the meat and bring to the boil uncovered. Skim off any foam that rises, then immediately lower the heat, cover the pot, and simmer for 1½ hours.

Make a sauce by whisking together the oil, vinegar, and a little salt and pepper. Just before serving sprinkle in the chopped chervil.

First, serve a bowl of the bouillon as a soup, with slices of brown bread. Then serve the different meats, sliced and arranged on a hot platter, with the sauce in a sauceboat on the side.

Serving suggestion: Thirty minutes before the meat has finished cooking, take some of the cooking liquid out of the pot and use it to make Rice Pilaf (p. 224). Serve at the same time as the meat.

Note: A very small turkey is called for in this recipe; if you can't find one, use turkey legs only, or buy a large turkey and use 1 breast and 1 leg, cut apart (the other half of the turkey can be cut into pieces and used to make the Cock in Red Wine (p. 149).

Save any leftover bouillon and use it in other recipes. Ed.

PHEASANT OR GUINEA HEN WITH CHESTNUTS
Poule faisane, ou faisan, ou pintadeau, aux marrons

PREPARATION TIME: 1 hour
COOKING TIME: pheasant 1 hour; guinea hen 45 minutes

INGREDIENTS FOR 3 TO 4 SERVINGS:
2¼ pounds (1 kg) chestnuts
Salt, pepper
3 to 4 thin rashers streaky bacon
A guinea hen or pheasant weighing 2 to 2½ pounds (900 g to 1.15 kg) prepared
    for roasting
1 ounce (30 g) butter (for the bird)
2½ ounces (70 g) butter (for the chestnuts)
4 tablespoons hot water

Begin by preparing the chestnuts: since peeling them takes quite a while, you might plan to do that the day before cooking.

All chestnuts have two skins, a hard outer one and a thin, furry inner one that clings to the nut. To remove the hard outer one make a slit in it with a sharp knife, then peel it off (be careful not to cut the chestnut in half when making the slit). Place the peeled chestnuts in a large saucepan, add enough water to cover, a little salt, then cover the pot and bring to the boil. Boil for 5 minutes, then remove the pot from the heat but leave the chestnuts in the hot water. With a slotted spoon, remove the chestnuts from the water 3 or 4 at a time, and rub or peel off the inner skin using a clean cloth or tea-towel (this must be done while the nuts are very hot). Leave the peeled chestnuts to cool, then place in a container, close tightly and put them in the refrigerator overnight; or use them right away if peeling them the same day you cook the bird.

Attach the bacon rashers to the bird, using string or toothpicks to hold them in place.

Melt 1 ounce (30 g) of butter in a pot large enough to hold the bird comfortably. Salt and pepper the bird, then brown in the butter over moderate heat for 10 minutes, turning frequently to brown evenly. Butter a piece of greaseproof paper slightly larger than the pot, place it over the pot buttered side down, then cover the pot and cook for about 40 minutes more, turning the bird once or twice.

Just before the bird has finished cooking melt the remaining 2½ ounces (70 g) butter in a high-sided frying pan and sauté the chestnuts for 10 minutes, gently shaking the pan frequently to roll them around in the butter and brown on all sides. Sprinkle with salt and pepper.

Either serve the bird whole or carve it, and place it on a hot platter surrounded by the chestnuts. Add the hot water to the pot the bird was cooked in, bring just to the boil, season with salt and pepper, and serve in a sauce-boat on the side.

GUINEA HEN OR PARTRIDGES WITH CABBAGE
Pintade ou perdrix au chou

PREPARATION TIME: 25 minutes
COOKING TIME: 30–45 minutes

INGREDIENTS FOR 4 SERVINGS:
1 green Savoy cabbage
3 carrots, peeled and quartered
5 ounces (150 g) bacon, diced
Bouquet garni, made of thyme and bay leaf
A 2- to 2½-pound (900-g to 1.15-kg) guinea hen; or 2 partridges or pigeons
2 thin slices fatty bacon or pork fat
Salt, pepper
3½ ounces (100 g) butter
4 fluid ounces (12 cl) hot water

Preheat the oven to 350°F (180°C or Mark 4).

Cut out the base of the cabbage, then cut it into quarters. Wash it under cold running water, then boil for 15 to 20 minutes in a large pot of lightly salted boiling water with the carrots, bacon, and the *bouquet garni*. Drain in a colander. Discard the *bouquet garni*.

Place just the cabbage in a roasting pan in the oven to dry out for 10 minutes, then remove from the oven and reserve with the bacon and carrots.

Clean the bird(s); if using freshly killed partridges, pluck them just before cooking. Cover the thighs and breast of each bird with the slices of pork fat or bacon and attach with kitchen string. Sprinkle generously with pepper, but salt lightly because of the pork.

Melt just over half the butter in a pot large enough to hold the bird(s) comfortably, and cook for 10 minutes, turning frequently to brown evenly. Cover the pot and finish cooking (20 to 25 minutes for the partridge, or 35 minutes for a guinea hen), turning from time to time. Remove the pot from the heat but leave the bird(s) inside, covered, for 5 minutes more.

Meanwhile, reheat the cabbage, carrots, and bacon by sautéing them together in a frying pan with the remaining butter.

To serve, lift the bird(s) out of the pot, discard the bacon, and carve.

154

Place on a hot platter, surrounded by the vegetables and bacon, and keep warm. Pour any carving juices into the pot, add the hot water, bring to the boil, season with a little pepper, then pour the sauce into a sauceboat and serve.

CAPON ROASTED WITH BLACK OLIVES

Chapon de Bresse rôti aux olives noires

PREPARATION TIME: 15 minutes
COOKING TIME: about 1½ hours

INGREDIENTS FOR 8 SERVINGS:
8 ounces (250 g) black olives
A 5½-pound (2½ kg) capon (see *Note*)
Salt, pepper
1½ ounces (40 g) butter, for the roasting pan
4 fluid ounces (12 cl) warm water
2 ounces (60 g) softened butter, cut into 10 pieces

Preheat the oven to 450°F (230°C or Mark 8).

Rinse the olives in cold running water and drain. Place them inside the capon, then sew up the bird to keep them inside while roasting. Sprinkle the capon with salt and pepper, place it in a generously buttered roasting pan, and roast for 1½ hours (about 17 minutes per pound). Baste after the first 15 minutes and every so often thereafter. Once the cooking time is up, turn off the oven but leave the bird inside for another 10 minutes before serving.

To serve, lift the capon out of the roasting pan and carve; save any juices that come from it for the sauce. Place the olives in a bowl. Add the warm water and any carving juices to the roasting pan, place over high heat, and add the softened butter. Bring to the boil, whisking constantly; when all the butter has melted, add salt and pepper, then pour into a sauceboat.

Serve with the sauce and the olives on the side.

Serving suggestions: Serve with Sauté Potatoes (p. 201) or French Beans (p. 192).

Note: If a capon is unavailable, two 3-pound (1.4-kg) chickens may be used instead. Follow the directions given here but roast for only 50 minutes. Ed.

155

BREAST OF GUINEA HEN IN CREAM SAUCE
Suprême de pintadeau à la crème

PREPARATION TIME: 15 minutes
COOKING TIME: 1 hour

INGREDIENTS FOR 2 SERVINGS:
A 2¾ pound (1.25 kg) guinea hen (*or roasting chicken. Ed.*)
3½ pints (2 litres) water
Bouquet garni made with 1 small leek, 1 celery stalk, 1 sprig thyme and ¼ bay
    leaf tied together
4 carrots, peeled and sliced
4 tablespoons dry white wine (preferably Pouilly-Fuissé)
4 tablespoons port
Salt, pepper
5 peppercorns
8 ounces (250 g) large spinach leaves
1 slice ham off the bone – about 3½ ounces (100 g) – cut in half
1½ ounces (40 g) butter
6 tablespoons (10 cl) double cream

Only the breast meat from the guinea hen will be used in this recipe. The legs, however, will be cooked in making the stock; they can be saved and eaten cold with a salad on another occasion.

Begin by cutting off the legs, thighs and wings. Carefully cut the meat from each breast off in one piece and reserve. Cut the carcass, backbone and neck of the bird into large pieces and place in a pot with the legs, wings and water. Add the *bouquet garni* to the pot as well as the carrots, white wine, port, salt and peppercorns. Bring to the boil, skim, then lower the heat and simmer for 40 minutes, uncovered. Lift out the legs and keep for another meal, then strain the remaining liquid and place it back in the pot.

Wash the spinach leaves, drop them into a pot of lightly salted boiling water, bring back to the boil and boil slowly for 3 minutes. Lift the leaves out of the water with a slotted spoon and spread them out on a towel to dry, being careful not to tear them.

Split open each piece of breast meat lengthwise, cutting almost through the centre so that they will open like a book. Season with salt and pepper, then lay half of the ham on each breast and fold it closed inside. Salt and pepper again. Carefully wrap each piece of breast meat in spinach leaves, place half the butter on each one, wrap each one in a large piece of clear plastic wrap, going around it several times, then twist the ends once and fold them over to enclose the meat inside.

156

Heat the meat stock prepared earlier, then drop in the breasts and poach for 10 minutes at a gentle boil, turning them over after 5 minutes. Lift out, drain and reserve.

Boil 12 fluid ounces (35 cl) of the remaining liquid in a frying pan until it is thick and syrupy (draw lines through it with a wooden spoon – when the pan remains visible for a second or two, the liquid is thick enough). Stir in the cream, add salt and pepper if needed, and heat until almost boiling.

Remove the plastic wrap from around each breast then place them (still wrapped in the spinach) in the sauce and simmer for 2 minutes (do not boil). Place each breast in the centre of a hot dinner plate, pour the sauce around them and serve immediately.

VARIATION: The breasts can simply be wrapped in plastic wrap without being wrapped in spinach; or cabbage leaves, which are much easier to work with, can be used instead of spinach.

RABBIT LYONS-STYLE
Lapin sauté à la lyonnaise

PREPARATION TIME: 30 minutes
COOKING TIME: about 50 minutes

INGREDIENTS FOR 4 SERVINGS:
A 3-pound (1.4-kg) rabbit, cut into 10 pieces
Salt, pepper
3 ounces (75 g) butter
4 shallots, peeled and chopped
2 cloves garlic, whole and unpeeled
5 ounces (150 g) bacon, cut into ½ inch (1 cm) cubes
Bouquet garni made of thyme, bay leaf and parsley
1 pound (500 g) tomatoes, peeled and coarsely chopped
1 ounce (30 g) butter (for the mushrooms)
8 ounces (250 g) fresh mushrooms, cleaned and quartered
4 fluid ounces (12 cl) dry white wine

Salt and pepper the rabbit.

Melt 3 ounces (75 g) of butter in a large high-sided frying pan. When it foams, add the rabbit, shallots, garlic, bacon and *bouquet garni* and cook for 10 minutes, turning frequently to brown evenly. Add the tomatoes and cook very slowly, uncovered, for 25 minutes, turning 3 to 4 times. While the rabbit is cooking melt 1 ounce (30 g) of butter in a small frying pan, add the mushrooms and sauté until all their moisture has evaporated and they begin to brown. Lift them out of the pan and add them to the rabbit.

When the 25 minutes' cooking time is up for the rabbit, add the white wine, stirring to detach any meat juices; cover and cook for 8 minutes more over very low heat. Taste for salt and pepper, then remove the pan from the heat and leave the rabbit 5 minutes longer in the pan before serving.

Place the rabbit in a hot serving dish, pour over the sauce and serve.

Serving suggestions: Serve with Mashed Potatoes (p. 204) or pasta.

Note: A chicken the same size as the rabbit can be cut into pieces and cooked in the same way. Ed.

RABBIT SAUTÉED WITH DIJON MUSTARD
Lapin à la moutarde

PREPARATION TIME: 20 minutes
COOKING TIME: about 50 minutes

INGREDIENTS FOR 4 SERVINGS:
1 3-pound (1.4-kg) rabbit, cut into 10
  pieces
Salt, pepper
5 ounces (150 g) Dijon mustard
3 ounces (75 g) butter
4 ounces (125 g) bacon, diced
8 ounces (250 g) baby onions, peeled
Bouquet garni, made of thyme, bay
  leaf, and parsley tied together

3 cloves garlic, whole and unpeeled
9 fluid ounces (25 cl) dry white wine
6 medium mushrooms, cleaned and
  quartered
6 tablespoons (10 cl) double cream
1 tablespoon lemon juice

Fresh Dijon mustard is essential for this recipe; buy a new jar the day you cook the rabbit.

Season the pieces of rabbit with salt and pepper, then use a spoon to coat them on all sides with the mustard.

Heat the butter in a high-sided frying pan. When it begins to foam, add the rabbit, bacon, onions, *bouquet garni* and garlic. Brown over high heat, turning frequently, for 20 minutes. Add the wine, scraping the bottom of the pan to dissolve any juices stuck to it, and the mushrooms. Cook over moderately low heat for 10 minutes, lower the heat, cover, and simmer very slowly for 15 minutes more to finish cooking.

Lift the pieces of rabbit, the onions, and bacon out of the pan with a slotted spoon and place them on a hot platter. Discard the *bouquet garni*. Whisk the cream into the pan juices (if all the wine has evaporated, add 6 tablespoons (10 cl) of water as well), heat until almost boiling, then stir in the lemon juice. Remove from the heat, add salt and pepper if needed, spoon over the rabbit, and serve immediately.

Serving suggestion: This is excellent with pasta.

Note: A chicken of the same weight can be cut into pieces and cooked exactly as described above. For a more pronounced mustard taste, save a generous tablespoon of mustard and, just before serving, stir it into the sauce away from the heat. Ed.

RABBIT PÂTÉ
Rillettes de lapin

PREPARATION TIME: 30 minutes (plus time to marinate)
COOKING TIME: 1½ hours (plus time to chill)

INGREDIENTS FOR 6 TO 8 SERVINGS:
1 2¾-pound (1.25-kg) rabbit
1 pound (500 g) pig's cheek, cut into 8 to 10 pieces
Salt, pepper
3 onions, peeled and quartered
3 carrots, peeled and quartered
Bouquet garni, made of 2 celery stalks, 1 sprig thyme, ¼ bay leaf, and 3 sprigs
   parsley, tied together
5 peppercorns
1 tablespoon olive oil
1 bottle dry white wine
3½ ounces (100 g) lard

Cut the rabbit into 6 pieces at the joints in order not to splinter the bones. Place in a large bowl with the pork, salt, and pepper, then add the carrots, onions and the *bouquet garni*. Stir in the peppercorns, oil and wine, then leave to marinate for 6 hours or overnight before cooking.

Lift the rabbit and pork out of the marinade and pat dry with kitchen paper. Heat the lard in a large pot over moderate heat (the pot should be wide enough for all the meat to sit on the bottom without piling up). Cook the rabbit and pork for 10 minutes to brown lightly, turning frequently, then pour all the marinade ingredients into the pot (the liquid should barely cover the meat). Bring to the boil, then lower the heat and cook at a slow boil, uncovered, for about 1½ hours. Measure the liquid in the pot occasionally by straining it into a measuring cup; when the cooking is done, there should be ½ pint (25 cl) of liquid left.

Lift the rabbit and pork out of the pan. Use two forks to shred the meat (discard the bones) by holding the meat with one fork and pulling at it with the other fork. Place the shredded meat into a salad bowl. Season with salt and pepper, add the strained cooking liquid, and refrigerate overnight before serving.

Serving suggestions: Serve with bread and a Green Salad (p. 66), or pickled gherkins.

HARE STEWED IN RED WINE
Lapin en civet ou civet de lièvre

PREPARATION TIME: 20 minutes
COOKING TIME: 1 hour

INGREDIENTS FOR 6 TO 8 SERVINGS:
A 5½ to 6½ pound (2.5 to 3 kg) hare or rabbit
Blood from the animal (see *Note* to recipe for Cock in Red Wine p. 149)
1 teaspoon vinegar (if using blood)
Salt, pepper
1 clove garlic, peeled and finely chopped
2 tablespoons finely chopped parsley
3 tablespoons brandy
3½ ounces (100 g) butter
1 bottle red wine (preferably Burgundy)
2 tablespoons (20 g) flour
4 tablespoons (6 cl) hot water
Bouquet garni made with 2 sprigs parsley, 1 sprig thyme, ¼ bay leaf, 1 celery
    stalk, and the white of 1 leek, tied together
1 clove garlic, peeled but whole
1 ounce (20 g) softened butter (for the *beurre manié*)
2 tablespoons (20 g) flour (for the *beurre manié*)

If possible, use a freshly killed animal and save the blood (mixed with a teaspoon of vinegar) for making the sauce (see *Note* of the Cock with Red Wine recipe, p. 149). Save the liver, heart and lungs for the sauce as well.

Cut the rabbit or hare into 8 to 10 pieces. Season with salt and pepper.

Chop the liver, heart and lungs, mix them with the garlic, chopped parsley and brandy, season with salt and pepper and reserve.

Melt the butter in a pot large enough to hold the rabbit comfortably. When the butter starts to foam add the pieces of rabbit and cook for 20 minutes turning frequently to brown on all sides.

In a saucepan, bring the red wine to a boil. Stir the flour into the pot with the rabbit, stir in the hot water to bind the sauce, then pour in the boiling red wine. Add the *bouquet garni*, and the whole garlic, bring to the boil, then immediately lower the heat and boil slowly, uncovered, for 25 minutes. At the end of this time place over very low heat (use a heat diffuser if you have one) and simmer very slowly for 10 minutes more.

Make a *beurre manié* by mixing together the butter and flour with your fingers. Reserve for thickening the sauce if necessary. Lift the pieces of rabbit out of the pot and place in a hot serving dish. Keep warm while making the sauce.

161

Strain the cooking liquid and put back into the pot over moderate heat. Mix the blood with the liver-brandy mixture, stir in a little of the cooking liquid, then pour into the pot, stirring. Heat until the sauce thickens, stirring constantly, but do not allow to boil. If you feel the sauce should be thicker, whisk in the *beurre manié*, broken into small pieces. When smooth, pour the sauce over the rabbit and serve.

Serving suggestions: This dish can be made a day in advance and reheated – it's even better. In this case, don't add the blood and liver until just before serving. (If you have some left over, and wish to reheat it with the blood already in it, heat, stirring constantly, and do not allow to boil.) Serve with pasta, a chestnut purée, or celery purée.

HARE OR VENISON IN MUSTARD SAUCE
Râble de lièvre, ou selle de chevreuil, à la moutarde

PREPARATION TIME: 20 minutes
COOKING TIME: 20–40 minutes

INGREDIENTS FOR 4 TO 6 SERVINGS:
2 saddle of hare weighing about 14 ounces (400 g) each, *or* 1 saddle of venison
    weighing about 1¾ pound (800 g)
Salt, pepper
3½ ounces (100 g) Dijon mustard
3½ ounces (100 g) butter
Bouquet garni, made with thyme and bay leaf
2 cloves garlic, whole and unpeeled
9 fluid ounces (25 cl) dry white wine
7 fluid ounces (20 cl) double cream

Season the meat with salt and pepper, then rub it on all sides with the mustard.

Heat the butter in a high-sided frying pan until it foams, then add the meat, *bouquet garni*, and garlic. Cook hare for a total of 20 minutes, venison 40 minutes, over moderate heat, turning once.

Lift the meat out of the pan and place on a hot platter. Stir in the wine over high heat, scraping the bottom of the pan to dissolve any meat juices stuck to it. Stir in the cream and lower the heat (the sauce should be very hot, but the cream should not boil). Remove the *bouquet garni*, season with salt and pepper if needed, spoon the sauce over the meat, and serve.

Serving suggestions: This is delicious with the Potato Crêpe (p. 205) or Chanterelles (p. 174).

162

8

OFFAL

Offal is not sufficiently appreciated. This is a shame because it is generally inexpensive and delicious if properly prepared. Like any other meat, offal should be left at room temperature for an hour before cooking.

CALF'S LIVER
Rôti de foie de veau

PREPARATION TIME: 15 minutes
COOKING TIME: 30 minutes (plus 15 minutes resting time)

INGREDIENTS FOR 4 TO 6 SERVINGS:
A piece of calf's liver weighing 1¾ to 2¼ pounds (800 g to 1 kg)
Salt, pepper
2 ounces (60 g) butter
4 carrots, peeled and quartered
4 onions, peeled and quartered
Bouquet garni made of thyme, bay leaf and a stalk of celery
5 tablespoons dry white wine
5 tablespoons water

Salt and pepper the calf's liver on all sides. In a pot, melt the butter, then add the liver, carrots, onions and *bouquet garni*; brown the liver over moderate heat for about 10 minutes, turning frequently. Add the wine and water, heat almost to boiling, then cover the pot and simmer for 20 minutes. Remove the pot from the heat, season with a little salt and pepper, cover the pot again and leave to rest for 15 minutes away from the heat before serving.

To serve, lift the liver out of the pot, slice it on a board, then place the slices on a hot serving platter. Pour any juices that come from the liver back into the pot. Bring to a boil (you can add a little hot water if you feel there won't be enough sauce), then strain over the liver and serve immediately, with the carrots and onions in a dish on the side, or arranged around the liver on the platter.

Serving suggestions: Serve with Spinach (p. 181) or Braised Lettuce (p. 185).

BRAISED TONGUE
Langue de bœuf braisée

PREPARATION TIME: 50 minutes (plus 2 hours soaking)
COOKING TIME: 2–2½ hours

INGREDIENTS FOR 6 TO 8 SERVINGS:
1 ox tongue – about 4-pound (1.6-kg), roots removed
Salt, pepper
7 ounces (200 g) butter
12 baby onions, peeled
4 medium carrots, peeled, quartered, and cut into thick sticks
5 ounces (150 g) bacon, cut into ½ inch (1 cm) cubes
1 tablespoon (10 g) flour
8 fluid ounces (25 cl) dry white wine
1¼ pint (75 cl) bouillon (see French Boiled Dinner, p. 118) or hot water
2 veal bones
Bouquet garni, made of 2 sprigs thyme, 4 sprigs parsley, ½ bay leaf, and 1
   celery stalk tied together
1 tablespoon tomato purée

Leave the tongue in a large bowl of cold water for 2 hours; then drain it, place it in a pot, add 5 pints (3 litres) fresh cold water, the salt, and bring to a boil. Skim off any foam that surfaces and boil the tongue for 10 minutes. Place it in a colander and hold under cold running water until cool enough to handle. Use a paring knife to scrape off the thick skin that surrounds the tongue (a thin white film will be left in most places), then dry it with kitchen paper.

Melt the butter in a pot just large enough to hold the tongue comfortably. Add the carrots, onions, and bacon, and cook for about 3 minutes or until the vegetables begin to soften. Place the tongue in the pot and brown on all sides over moderate heat for about 10 minutes. Sprinkle in the flour, stir to combine, then add the wine, stirring constantly. Add the bouillon or hot water, the veal bones and the *bouquet garni*; the tongue should be about half covered by the liquid. Season with salt and pepper, bring just to the boil, then immediately lower the heat, cover the pot, and simmer slowly at least 2 hours. Turn the tongue over 5 or 6 times while cooking. After 2 hours test by piercing it with a long skewer. If the skewer goes into the tongue with virtually no resistance, it is done.

To serve, remove the tongue from the sauce, stir in the tomato purée, and simmer while slicing the tongue. Place the tongue on a hot platter.

164

To the sauce add any juices that came from it while slicing, spoon a little sauce over the tongue and serve, with a sauceboat of the sauce on the side.

Serving suggestions: Serve with Rice (p. 217) or boiled potatoes and butter.

VEAL KIDNEYS IN MUSTARD SAUCE
Rognons de veau en cocotte

PREPARATION TIME: 15 minutes
COOKING TIME: about 10 minutes

INGREDIENTS FOR 6 SERVINGS:
3 veal kidneys weighing about 12 ounces (350 g) each
Salt, pepper
2 ounces (60 g) butter
3 shallots, peeled and chopped
4 tablespoons brandy
6 tablespoons (10 cl) double cream
1 tablespoon Dijon mustard

Remove all the fat and gristle from the kidneys. Cut them into thin slices, then sprinkle with salt and pepper.

Melt the butter in a frying pan; when it starts to foam, add the kidneys and sauté over high heat for 6 to 8 minutes, shaking the pan frequently so the slices will cook on all sides.

Lift the slices out of the pan with a slotted spoon. Place on a hot platter and keep warm while making the sauce.

Add the shallots to the pan the kidneys were cooked in, stir over high heat until soft, then stir in first the brandy, then the cream, scraping the bottom of the pan to dissolve any meat juices, and finally the mustard. Spoon the sauce over the kidneys immediately and serve.

Serving suggestions: Serve with Rice (p. 217) or Spinach (p. 181).

BRAINS WITH CAPERS
Cervelles meunières

PREPARATION TIME: 20 minutes (plus soaking overnight)
COOKING TIME: 30 minutes

INGREDIENTS FOR 4 SERVINGS:
4 lambs' brains
2 carrots, peeled and quartered
2 onions, peeled and halved
Bouquet garni made with 2 sprigs parsley, 2 celery stalks, 1 sprig thyme, and 1
   bay leaf tied together
6⅓ cups (1½ litres) water
2 tablespoons (20 g) flour
2 ounces (60 g) butter
1½ ounces (40 g) capers (or more, to taste)
Salt, pepper

Place the brains in a large bowl of cold water overnight in the refrigerator before cooking.

Remove from the refrigerator 2 hours before cooking, but leave in the water. Just before cooking hold each brain under cold running water and take off the thin membrane that surrounds it. Leave to drain in a colander. In a large pot, place the carrots, onions, and *bouquet garni*; add the water and bring to the boil. As soon as the water boils add the brains, lower the heat and poach for 10 minutes, then lift the brains out of the pot and place in a strainer above a mixing bowl to cool. Keep any juices that fall into the bowl, measure them and add enough of the cooking liquid to bring the total to 6 tablespoons. Reserve.

When the brains are cold cut them into thin slices and roll them in the flour, shaking off as much excess as possible.

Heat the butter in a large frying pan; when it starts to foam add the sliced brains and brown for about 5 minutes on each side. When brown add the capers, sprinkle with salt and pepper, then place the brains on hot dinner plates. Add the reserved cooking liquid to the pan, scraping to dissolve anything stuck to the bottom, then pour over the brains and serve immediately.

Serving suggestions: Serve with boiled potatoes or pasta.

9

VEGETABLES

Some of the recipes in this chapter could be served as lunches or light meals, especially the stuffed vegetables – tomatoes, courgettes, etc.

Vary the vegetables you serve, and always buy them fresh. Buy what is in season, and everything you make will taste better. Wash vegetables under cold running water; never leave them to soak, as they lose both vitamins and taste this way.

CARROTS AND PEAS
Carottes-petits pois

PREPARATION TIME: 15 minutes
COOKING TIME: 40 minutes

INGREDIENTS FOR 4 SERVINGS:
1½ ounces (40 g) butter
4 large carrots, peeled and cut into thick sticks 2 inches (5 cm) long
8 baby onions, peeled
Bouquet garni, made with thyme and bay leaf
1 pound (500 g) shelled peas – buy 3¼ pounds (1.25 kg) if in pod
Salt, pepper
1 teaspoon granulated sugar

Melt the butter in a high-sided frying pan, add the carrots and onions, and simmer for about 5 minutes, stirring occasionally. Pour in enough water to barely cover, add the *bouquet garni*, and cook for 20 minutes. Add the peas, salt, pepper, and sugar (add more water if necessary so that the peas will be barely covered). Bring to the boil, cover the pan, lower the heat, and simmer for 20 minutes more, stirring from time to time. Remove the *bouquet garni*, then serve in a dish or on a platter with meat.

CARDOONS AU GRATIN
Gratin de cardons

PREPARATION TIME: 20 minutes
COOKING TIME: 45 minutes

INGREDIENTS FOR 4 SERVINGS:
2 small cardoons
18 fluid ounces (50 cl) milk
4½ pints (2½ litres) water (for the
    cardoons)
Salt
2 marrow bones
18 fluid ounces (50 cl) water (for the
    marrow bones)
⅔ ounce (20 g) butter (for the dish)
4 ounces (125 g) grated gruyère
    cheese
1 ounce (30 g) butter (for the sauce)
1 tablespoon flour

The cardoon is a relative of the artichoke that looks rather like a large head of celery; unfortunately it isn't found everywhere, nor at all seasons. A winter vegetable, it is best from November to February. When you buy them, pick those which are small and dull white in colour – they are generally the most tender.

Peeling the cardoons is a time-consuming process that requires great care. Cut off the hollow ends of the stalks and remove all the strings, as you would with celery. Cut the remaining (solid) part of the stalks into pieces about 2¼ inches (3 cm) long; the base, where all the stalks are joined together, can simply be sliced – this is the best part to my mind. Wash under cold running water and drain.

Heat the milk and water in a large pot until boiling, add salt and the cardoons, partially cover the pot and cook for 15 to 20 minutes. Lower the heat if it looks as if the milk is rising and will overflow.

Preheat the oven to 350°F (180°C or Mark 4).

While the cardoons are cooking, poach the marrow bones. Place them in a small saucepan, add the cold water, salt lightly and heat almost to boiling. Simmer for 10 minutes. Lift the bones out of the pot with a slotted spoon and take out the marrow; cut it into thick slices and reserve. Save 9 fluid ounces (25 cl) of the water the bones cooked in for later use.

168

Butter a small baking dish. Drain the cardoons, then put them in the dish and sprinkle them with the grated cheese.

Melt the butter in a saucepan, stir in the flour and cook until it starts to change colour, then, little by little, stir in the reserved marrow-bone water. Boil until the sauce is just thick enough to coat a spoon.

Place the slices of marrow on the cardoons, pour over the sauce, bake for 25 minutes or until beginning to brown and serve.

BABY ARTICHOKES "BARIGOULE"
Artichauts "barigoule"

PREPARATION TIME: 20 minutes
COOKING TIME: about 45 minutes

INGREDIENTS FOR 4 SERVINGS:
4½ pints (2½ litres) water
8 baby artichokes, about 1¼ pounds (660 g)
3 tablespoons olive oil
4 large tomatoes, peeled and chopped
4 medium mushrooms, cleaned and quartered
8 baby onions, peeled
2 cloves garlic, whole and unpeeled
1 sprig thyme
¼ bay leaf
4 ounces (125 g) bacon, diced
Salt, pepper

Bring the water to the boil in a large pot.

Cut off the leaves of each artichoke about a third of the way down from the top. Cut off the stems, then remove the tough outer leaves around the base and cut each artichoke into four pieces. Use a little spoon to scoop out the choke in the centre of each piece. Quickly rinse the artichokes in warm water, then drop them into the boiling water, cook for 15 minutes, and drain.

Heat the oil in a high-sided frying pan or cast-iron pot. Add the tomatoes, mushrooms, onions, garlic, thyme, bay leaf, and bacon. Cook for 10 to 20 minutes, or until half the moisture from the vegetables has evaporated, then add the artichokes, salt, and pepper. Cover the pan and simmer for 25 minutes.

Serve immediately, either in the pan or in a serving dish.

Note: Artichokes cooked this way are excellent cold as well as hot. Ed.

169

GLAZED CARROTS AND TURNIPS
Carottes et navets glacés

PREPARATION TIME: 15 minutes
COOKING TIME: 30 minutes

INGREDIENTS FOR 4 SERVINGS:
1 pound (500 g) baby carrots, peeled and halved
1 pound (500 g) baby turnips, peeled and halved
2 ounces (60 g) butter
1 dessertspoon (15 g) granulated sugar
Salt, pepper

Boil the carrots and turnips in a large pot of lightly salted water for 8 to 10 minutes, then drain.

Melt the butter in a high-sided frying pan, add the vegetables, and cook over moderate heat for 10 to 15 minutes to dry out and coat with butter; shake the pan frequently while the vegetables are cooking.

Lower the heat, sprinkle in the sugar, and cook, shaking the pan, until the sugar coats the vegetables and begins to brown. Season with salt and pepper, and serve.

Serving suggestion: Serve as garnish with meat.

CREAMED CELERIAC
Céleri-rave à la crème

PREPARATION TIME: 15 minutes
COOKING TIME: 30 minutes

INGREDIENTS FOR 4 SERVINGS:
1 celeriac (root celery) weighing about 1 pound (500 g), peeled and diced
2 medium potatoes, peeled and diced
Salt
6 tablespoons (10 cl) double cream
Pepper
1 ounce (30 g) butter

Rinse the diced vegetables under cold running water. Place in a saucepan, pour in enough cold water to cover, add salt, bring to the boil, and cook for 30 minutes.

Drain, then immediately purée the vegetables in a food mill with a medium grill or use a potato masher. Place in a hot serving dish. Whisk in the cream, add pepper, and salt if necessary. Stir in the butter and serve.

Serving suggestion: Serve with either meat or fish.

MIXED VEGETABLES
Jardinière de légumes

PREPARATION TIME: about 30 minutes
COOKING TIME: 35 minutes

INGREDIENTS FOR 6 TO 8 SERVINGS:
6 to 8 baby onions, peeled
1½ pounds (700 g) potatoes, peeled and diced
5 medium carrots, peeled and cut into thick sticks
Bouquet garni, made with thyme and bay leaf
4 ounces (125 g) lean bacon, diced
14 ounces (400 g) shelled peas – buy 2 pounds (900 g) if in pod
8 lettuce leaves
Salt, pepper
2 ounces (50 g) butter

Bring a large saucepan of salted water to a boil and add the onions, potatoes, carrots, and *bouquet garni*. Cover and boil gently for about 20 minutes, then add the bacon, peas, and lettuce, and cook for 15 minutes uncovered.

To serve, drain the vegetables, discard the *bouquet garni*, and place in a hot serving dish. Season with salt and pepper, stir in the butter, and serve immediately.

MUSHROOMS IN CREAM AU GRATIN
Champignons à la crème

PREPARATION TIME: 20 minutes
COOKING TIME: 30 minutes

INGREDIENTS FOR 4 SERVINGS:
1 pound 10 ounces (750 g) mushrooms
2 ounces (50 g) butter
3 egg yolks
6 tablespoons (10 cl) double cream
Salt, pepper
Nutmeg
2 ounces (60 g) grated gruyère cheese

The mushrooms can be young "button" ones or older ones which have more flavour, but in either case they should be fresh, unbruised and uniformly coloured. Cut off any dirt on the stems, wash rapidly under cold running water, then either slice or quarter depending on their size.

Preheat the oven to 350°F (180°C or Mark 4).

Melt the butter in a saucepan, add the mushrooms and cook slowly, stirring frequently, for 15 minutes or until all the water they give out has evaporated and only butter is left in the pan.

Lightly butter a small baking dish, then pour in the mushrooms. Whisk the egg yolks and cream together, season with salt, pepper and a little nutmeg, then pour over the mushrooms. Sprinkle with the grated cheese, then bake for 15 to 20 minutes or until beginning to brown. Serve the mushrooms hot from the oven in the dish they were cooked in.

CHANTERELLES
Girolles ou chanterelles

PREPARATION TIME: 15 minutes
COOKING TIME: 20 minutes

INGREDIENTS FOR 4 SERVINGS:
1¾ pound (800 g) fresh chanterelles
2 ounces (50 g) butter
Salt, pepper
1 clove garlic, peeled and coarsely crushed (optional)
1 shallot, peeled and finely chopped (optional)
2 tablespoons coarsely chopped parsley (optional)

Cut off the dirt from the base of each mushroom, then wash them quickly under cold running water and drain.

Melt the butter in a frying pan, add the mushrooms, and cook over moderate heat for approximately 20 minutes, or until all the water they give out has evaporated completely. Continue cooking until the mushrooms begin to brown. At this point, they are done (this method of cooking is good for almost all mushrooms).

Season the mushrooms with salt and pepper, and serve as they are. If you prefer, stir in garlic, shallots, or both, and sprinkle with parsley just before serving.

Serving suggestion: Chanterelles are marvellous served with Roast Veal with Olives (p. 125).

Note: Chanterelles are yellow-coloured wild mushrooms, not commercially available in Britain; ordinary button mushrooms will do perfectly well.

STUFFED CABBAGE
Chou farci

PREPARATION TIME: 35 minutes (plus 7 to 8 hours soaking time)
COOKING TIME: 2 hours

INGREDIENTS FOR 6 SERVINGS:
8 ounces (250 g) salt pork
1 green cabbage weighing about 2¼ pounds (1 kg), tough outer leaves
    removed
6 pints (3½ litres) water
Salt, pepper
8 fluid ounces (25 cl) milk
1 large onion, peeled and sliced
⅔ ounce (20 g) crumbled dry toast or melba toast
3 tablespoons chopped parsley
1 clove garlic, peeled and chopped
14 ounces (400 g) chopped leftover boiled beef (see French Boiled Dinner
    p. 118)
1 egg
2 ounces (50 g) butter
3 medium carrots, peeled and cut into thick strips
6 tablespoons (10 cl) water

Desalt the salt pork by soaking it 7 to 8 hours in cold water with ice cubes. Change the water once or twice.

Drain the pork and pat dry in a clean cloth, then cut off one slice and reserve. Place the rest of the pork in a saucepan, cover with cold water, bring to the boil, then lower the heat and simmer for 1 hour. Drain, cool, then chop it coarsely and reserve.

Once the salt pork has started cooking, cook the cabbage. Bring 6 pints (3½ litres) of water to the boil in a large pot and add a little salt. Turn the cabbage upside down and cut out the hard central core. Detach all the leaves and drop them into the boiling water, lower the heat, and simmer for 7 minutes. Drain and cool under cold running water, then place on a tea-towel to drain and dry.

In a small saucepan, bring the milk to the boil, add the onion and simmer for 8 minutes. Lift out the onion with a slotted spoon, chop coarsely, and reserve. Keep the milk.

Place the crumbled toast in a large bowl, pour in enough of the milk left from cooking the onion to barely cover, stir and allow to soak for about 10 to 15 minutes. Crush the toast using the prongs of a fork, then pour off any excess milk. Add the onion, parsley, garlic, chopped salt pork, and beef (see Comment). Stir in the egg, salt and pepper, and knead the stuffing with your hands to mix the ingredients perfectly together.

Preheat the oven to 350°F (180°C or Mark 4).

Melt the butter in a cast iron pot only slightly larger than the cabbage when it was whole. Add the carrots and the slice of uncooked salt pork reserved earlier. Cook until both begin to brown, then remove from the heat and leave to cool. When the pot is cool enough to touch, line the bottom (on top of the carrots and pork) and sides with about ⅔ of the cabbage leaves, allowing the ends of the leaves to drape over the sides of the pot a little. Pour the stuffing into the centre, cover with the remaining leaves, then fold in the cabbage leaves that drape over the sides to enclose the stuffing completely. Add the water, heat for 1 minute on top of the stove, then cover the pot and bake in the oven for 1 hour. Serve the cabbage hot from the oven in the pot it was cooked in.

COMMENT: All the ingredients for the stuffing can be worked through a meat grinder rather than chopped by hand, if preferred. In this case, the beef and salt pork can simply be cut into cubes, and the onion left in slices, before grinding. Use a large grill, since the stuffing shouldn't be chopped too fine.

CAULIFLOWER AU GRATIN
Gratin de chou-fleur

PREPARATION TIME: 15 minutes
COOKING TIME: 35 minutes

INGREDIENTS FOR 4 SERVINGS:
1 cauliflower weighing about 2 pounds (900 g)
5 pints (3 litres) water
Salt
1 tablespoon olive oil
1 stale breadcrust (optional)
8 fluid ounces (25 cl) milk
1 tablespoon (10 g) cornflour
6 tablespoons (10 cl) double cream
Salt, pepper
Nutmeg
2 ounces (50 g) grated gruyère cheese

Cut the central core from the cauliflower and separate the florets. Wash carefully in cold water.

Bring lightly salted water to the boil and add the oil; you can also add a stale breadcrust to the water (it will absorb some of the odour of the cauliflower as it cooks). Add the cauliflower, boil for 5 minutes from the time the water comes back to a boil, then drain. Butter a baking dish, place the cauliflower in it, and reserve.

Preheat the oven to 350°F (180°C or Mark 4).

Heat the milk in a saucepan. While it's heating, mix the cornflour with a tablespoon of cold water. Once the milk boils, remove the pot from the heat and stir in the cornflour mixture. Return to the heat and bring to the boil, stirring constantly. Cook until the sauce is thick enough to coat the spoon. Stir in the cream, salt, pepper, nutmeg, and grated cheese, then pour the sauce over the cauliflower and bake in the oven for 20 minutes, or until golden brown on top.

Serve straight from the baking dish.

CARROTS IN CREAM
Carottes à la crème

PREPARATION TIME: 15 minutes
COOKING TIME: 45 minutes

INGREDIENTS FOR 4 SERVINGS:
3 ounces (75 g) butter
2 pounds (900 g) carrots, peeled and cut into thick sticks 2 inches (5 cm) long
5 baby onions, peeled
Salt
1 teaspoon granulated sugar
2 tablespoons finely chopped parsley
6 tablespoons (10 cl) double cream

Melt the butter in a frying pan, add the carrots and onions, salt lightly, and sprinkle with sugar. Cover the pan and simmer for 40 minutes, stirring from time to time.

When the carrots have finished cooking, mix the parsley with the cream, pour on to the carrots, and cook for 5 minutes more, or until very hot (the cream should not boil). Serve immediately in a hot dish.

Serving suggestion: Carrots cooked this way are very good with roast veal.

BROCCOLI
Brocolis

PREPARATION TIME: 10 minutes
COOKING TIME: 10 minutes

INGREDIENTS FOR 3 TO 4 SERVINGS:
2¼ pounds (1 kg) broccoli
2 ounces (50 g) butter, *or* 7 fluid ounces (20 cl) double cream
Salt, pepper

If necessary, separate the broccoli into florets.

Bring a large pot of lightly salted water to the boil, then drop in the broccoli and boil for 7 to 10 minutes, or until tender but not soft. Lift the broccoli out and leave to drain for a few seconds on a clean cloth (be careful not to damage the florets which are quite fragile when cooked).

Place the broccoli in a hot serving dish and sprinkle with pepper. Then you can either pour a little melted butter over it, or cream that has been boiled until thick, or simply the juices from the meat it's being served with.

VARIATION: The broccoli can be boiled for only 2 or 3 minutes, to finish cooking in either the butter, cream, or meat juices. In this case, simmer slowly for 10 to 15 minutes more, gently shaking the pan frequently so as not to damage the broccoli (don't stir with a spoon). Add pepper, and serve.

Serving suggestions: Broccoli is delicious with the Fricassee of Scallops in Cream Sauce (p. 110). It is also excellent with meat or poultry.

SPINACH
Épinards

PREPARATION TIME: 15 minutes
COOKING TIME: about 15 minutes

INGREDIENTS FOR 4 SERVINGS:
6 pints (3½ litres) water
1 rounded tablespoon (30 g) coarse salt
3¼ pounds (1.5 kg) fresh spinach
2 ounces (50 g) butter
1 medium onion, peeled and sliced
Salt, pepper
2 tablespoons (10 cl) double cream

Bring the water and salt to the boil in a large pot.

While the water is heating up, carefully clean the spinach: remove the stalk and thick rib from each leaf, then wash in several changes of cold water. Carefully drain after washing, then drop the spinach little by little into the boiling water, pushing each addition into the water with a slotted spoon before adding more. Boil for 5 minutes from the time the water comes back to the boil (if you don't have a pot large enough to cook all the spinach at once, cook only as much as you can, remove from the pot with a slotted spoon, drain, cool under running water, and leave in the colander while cooking the rest).

When all the spinach is cooked, drain in a colander, cool immediately under cold running water, then squeeze out the water with your hands.

Melt the butter in a high-sided frying pan, brown the onion lightly, then add the spinach, salt, and pepper, and stir over moderate heat to heat thoroughly. Add the cream, cook for 5 minutes more, and serve immediately on a hot platter.

Serving suggestions: You can serve the spinach garnished with hard-boiled eggs cut in half and squares or triangles of bread fried in butter (croûtons), for a nice effect.

VARIATION: Fresh sorrel can be cooked in the same way.

STUFFED TOMATOES
Tomates farcies

PREPARATION TIME: 40 minutes (plus 7–8 hours soaking time)
COOKING TIME: about 2½ hours

INGREDIENTS FOR 6 SERVINGS:
7 ounces (200 g) salt pork
12 large tomatoes
1 sprig thyme
¼ bay leaf
Salt, pepper
4 small onions, peeled and sliced
8 fluid ounces (25 cl) milk
1 ounce (30 g) crumbled dry toast or
    melba toast
1 clove garlic, peeled and chopped
10 ounces (300 g) chopped leftover
    boiled beef or veal (see French
    Boiled Dinner p. 118, or Roast
    Veal with Olives p. 125)
2 tablespoons chopped parsley
1 egg
Salt, pepper
Nutmeg
2 ounces (60 g) butter (for the dish)

Soak the salt pork for 7–8 hours in cold water before cooking. To cook, rinse it in cold water, place in a saucepan, cover with cold water, bring to the boil, then lower the heat and simmer for about 1 hour. Drain and leave to cool before using to stuff the tomatoes.

Wash the tomatoes, then use a small knife to cut off the top third of each one. Reserve the tops. Use a spoon to scoop out the seeds and pulp from the centre of each tomato, being careful not to puncture the skins. Save the scooped-out pulp and seeds for making the sauce. Lightly salt the inside of each tomato and reserve.

Preheat the oven to 350°F (180°C or Mark 4).

Place the seeds and pulp in a small saucepan with a little thyme, bay leaf, salt, and pepper, and simmer for 15 to 20 minutes or until the consistency of a thin tomato sauce, stirring frequently. Reserve.

While the sauce is cooking, place the onions in a saucepan with the milk, bring to a boil, then lower the heat and simmer for 7 to 8 minutes. Lift the onions out of the milk with a slotted spoon and chop them coarsely. Save the milk.

(Continued p. 184)

Stuffed Tomatoes
Stuffed Courgettes (*recipe p. 188*)

Place the toast in a mixing bowl and add the milk used in cooking the onions. Allow to soak for about 10 minutes, then crush the toast with a fork; pour off any excess milk. Chop the salt pork, and add it to the toast along with the onion, garlic, leftover meat, and parsley (see Comment to the recipe for Stuffed Cabbage, pp. 175–6). Mix well, then add the egg, salt, pepper, and nutmeg, and knead with your hands to mix thoroughly.

Butter a baking dish just large enough to hold all the tomatoes. Fill each tomato with stuffing, then put the top sections back in place and arrange them in the baking dish. Pour the tomato sauce made earlier into the dish around the tomatoes, then place in the oven and bake for 1 hour. Serve hot from the oven in the baking dish.

Serving suggestion: Large tomatoes should be used. Since stuffed tomatoes are excellent reheated, don't be afraid of making more than you need.

TOMATOES PROVENÇALE-STYLE
Tomates provençales

PREPARATION TIME: 10 minutes
COOKING TIME: 25 minutes

INGREDIENTS FOR 4 SERVINGS:
4 large, ripe tomatoes
Salt
1 tablespoon finely chopped cilantro (Chinese parsley)
1 tablespoon finely chopped basil
2 tablespoons breadcrumbs
Pepper
2 cloves garlic, peeled and finely chopped
5 tablespoons (7.5 cl) olive oil

Preheat the oven to 450°F (230°C or Mark 8).

Wash the tomatoes, dry with a towel, then cut out the stems. Cut each tomato in half and place them in a baking dish, cut side up. Sprinkle generously with salt, then with the cilantro, basil, and breadcrumbs.

Dust with pepper, then place a little chopped garlic on top of each tomato half. Pour over the oil, and bake for 25 minutes. Serve hot from the oven in the baking dish.

Serving suggestion: Serve with either meat or fish.

184

BRAISED LETTUCE
Laitues braisées

PREPARATION TIME: 10 minutes
COOKING TIME: 20 minutes

INGREDIENTS FOR 4 SERVINGS:
4 small butterhead lettuces
2 ounces (50 g) butter
12 baby onions
Salt, pepper
2 egg yolks
6 tablespoons (10 cl) double cream

Remove any tough outer leaves from the lettuces and cut off the base of the stem. Leave the lettuces whole and gently wash them in cold water.

Melt the butter in a high-sided frying pan, add the onions, and brown lightly. Add the lettuces, salt, and pepper. Lower the heat, cover, and cook slowly for 15 to 20 minutes, or until tender, turning the lettuces occasionally.

While the lettuce is cooking, beat the egg yolks and cream together in a small mixing bowl. Season with salt and pepper.

When the lettuces are done, lift them out of the pan with a slotted spoon and place them on a hot platter. Keep warm. Remove the pan from the heat and pour the pan juices into the bowl with the egg-cream mixture, stirring constantly. Pour the sauce back into the pan and place over low heat, stirring constantly, just long enough for it to heat and thicken (do not allow to boil), then pour over the lettuces and serve.

Serving suggestion: Serve with any game bird.

COURGETTE FRITTERS
Beignets de courgettes

PREPARATION TIME: 20 minutes (plus 1½ hours resting time for the batter)
COOKING TIME: about 25 minutes

INGREDIENTS FOR 4 SERVINGS:
1 ounce (30 g) butter
4 ounces (125 cl) flour
1 teaspoon salt
8 fluid ounces (25 cl) pale ale
1 egg white
1 pound (500 g) courgettes (see Variations)
Oil for deep frying

To make the batter, melt the butter over very low heat or in a double boiler. Place the flour in a large mixing bowl, add the salt, then stir in the beer and melted butter. Beat to make a smooth batter; if lumps remain after beating, work the batter through a sieve to remove them. Place the batter in the refrigerator for 1½ hours. Just before using, beat the egg white until stiff and fold it into the batter.

Preheat the oven to 350°F (180°C or Mark 4).

Peel the courgettes and cut them into thin slices.

Heat the oil in a deep fryer; it should be no more than a third full. When a drop of water dropped into the oil evaporates, making a sharp, quick, pop, the oil is ready.

Coat 6 or 7 slices of courgette with the batter and drop them, one by one, into the hot oil. Cook until golden brown and floating on the surface of the oil. When done, lift them out of the oil with a slotted spoon, drain on paper towels, and place on a serving platter in the oven to keep warm (leave the door ajar so it doesn't become too hot). Cook the remaining batches of 6 or 7 slices each in the same way (when the oil has cooled completely, it can be strained, stored, and used again).

Serve as soon as the last batch is done.

Serving suggestion: Serve with leg of lamb.

VARIATIONS: If you grow your own courgettes, deep fry the flowers exactly as described here – they are delicious.

Aubergine or salsify (vegetable oyster) can also be cooked as described above (oyster plant should be cut into 2-inch (5-cm) pieces, boiled, and cooled before being dipped into the batter and fried).

Courgette Fritters

STUFFED COURGETTES
Courgettes farcies
Photo page 183

PREPARATION TIME: 2½ hours (plus 7 to 8 hours soaking time)
COOKING TIME: 1 hour 45 minutes

INGREDIENTS FOR 4 SERVINGS:
8 ounces (250 g) salt pork
4 large courgettes
⅔ ounce (20 g) crumbled dry toast or melba toast
5 fluid ounces (15 cl) milk
8 ounces (250 g) leftover cooked veal (see French Boiled Dinner p. 118, or
     Roast Veal with Olives p. 125)
1 clove garlic, peeled and chopped
4 small onions, peeled and chopped
2 tablespoons chopped parsley
1 egg
Nutmeg
4 fluid ounces (12 cl) Tomato Sauce (p. 90)
½ teaspoon dried thyme
¼ bay leaf, crumbled
Salt, pepper
2 ounces (50 g) grated gruyère cheese
2 ounces (50 g) butter
6 tablespoons (10 cl) water

Soak the salt pork in a large bowl of cold water for 7 to 8 hours before cooking (change the water several times). To cook, place it in a saucepan, add cold water to cover, bring to a boil, then lower the heat and simmer for 1 hour. Drain and cool before using to make the stuffing (the pork may be cooked in advance and kept in the refrigerator until ready to use).

Remove the stems from the courgettes, then wash them and wipe them dry, but do not peel. Cut each one in half lengthwise, then scoop out all the seeds, being careful not to puncture the skins. Reserve.

Preheat the oven to 350°F (180°C or Mark 4).

Place the toast in a mixing bowl, add the milk and allow to soak for about 10 minutes, then crush it with a fork and pour off any excess milk. Chop the salt pork and add it to the bread along with the veal, garlic, onions and parsley (see Comment to the recipe for Stuffed Cabbage p. 176). Stir in the egg, nutmeg, tomato sauce, thyme, bay leaf, salt and pepper. Mix well, then fill each half courgette with stuffing.

Place the courgettes in a large roasting pan, sprinkle with the cheese, add the water, dot with the butter and bake in the oven for 45 minutes Serve on a hot serving platter.

Serving suggestion: Stuffed courgettes can make a whole meal, especially if you serve them with Rice (p. 217).

CHICORY WITH HAM
Endives au jambon

PREPARATION TIME: 20 minutes
COOKING TIME: 50 minutes

INGREDIENTS FOR 4 SERVINGS:
2¼ pounds (1 kg) Belgian chicory
2½ pints (1½ litres) water
1½ teaspoons (10 g) salt
Juice of ½ lemon
⅔ ounce (20 g) butter (for the baking dish)
4 slices ham, cut into thin strips
6 fluid ounces (20 cl) double cream
3½ ounces (100 g) grated gruyère cheese
Pepper

Preheat the oven to 350°F (180°C or Mark 4).
Use a small knife to hollow out the base of each piece of chicory, then rinse them off under hot water.
Bring the water, salt and lemon juice to the boil, add the chicory, cook for 20 minutes, and drain.
Place the chicory in a buttered baking dish and sprinkle the strips of ham over. Pour in the cream and spread it out evenly. Sprinkle with the grated cheese and a little pepper, then bake for 25 to 30 minutes, or until golden brown.
Serve the chicory in the baking dish.

LEEKS AU GRATIN
Gratin de poireaux

PREPARATION TIME: 15 minutes
COOKING TIME: 1 hour

INGREDIENTS FOR 4 SERVINGS:
2¼ pounds (1 kg) large leeks
4½ pints (2½ litres) water
1 tablespoon salt
1 tablespoon cornflour
9 fluid ounces (25 cl) milk
Salt, pepper
Nutmeg
2 ounces (60 g) butter
6 tablespoons (10 cl) double cream
4 ounces (125 g) grated gruyère cheese

Cut the roots from each leek, then cut off about the top third of the green and discard. Slit open each leek lengthwise starting about an inch into the white and drawing the tip of the knife through to the end of the green. Wash each leek carefully, separating the leaves to remove any dirt, then cut each one in half, separating the green from the white. Tie the green together with kitchen string.

Preheat the oven to 450°F (230°C or Mark 8).

Bring the water and salt to the boil in a large pot and add the leeks; cook for 20 minutes, or until tender, from the time the water returns to the boil. Drain and remove the string.

Dissolve the cornflour with a tablespoon of cold water. Bring the milk to the boil in a saucepan and add the cornflour, stirring constantly. Cook for a minute or two, or until thick enough to coat the spoon. Remove from the heat, whisk in the cream, and season with salt, pepper, and nutmeg.

Butter a baking dish with half the butter, then place the leeks in it, alternating the white and green. Pour over the sauce, sprinkle with the grated cheese, and dot with the remaining butter. Bake for 25 minutes, or until golden brown on top. Serve in the baking dish.

Serving suggestion: Serve with roast pork.

FRENCH BEANS
Haricots verts

PREPARATION TIME: 15 minutes
COOKING TIME: about 15 minutes

INGREDIENTS FOR 4 SERVINGS:
5 pints (3 litres) water
1 tablespoon (25 g) salt
2 pounds (900 g) French beans
2 ounces (50 g) butter
Salt, pepper
Lemon juice (optional)

Bring the water and salt to the boil in a large pot.

In the meantime, top and tail the beans. Drop them into the boiling water and boil rapidly, uncovered, for 8 to 12 minutes, depending on size and how you like them. Use a slotted spoon to push down any beans that stick out of the water.

Fill a large basin or bowl with cold water and a tray of ice cubes. When the beans are done (taste one – you may want to cook them longer), drain them and drop them immediately into the ice water. Leave for 3 minutes, then lift out and drain completely.

Just before serving, melt the butter in a large frying pan, add the beans, season with salt and pepper, and warm over low heat, shaking the pan frequently. Serve as soon as the beans are hot. If you like, you can sprinkle them with a little lemon juice just before serving.

HARICOT BEANS PROVENÇALE
Haricots blancs à la provençale

PREPARATION TIME: 15 minutes (plus soaking time)
COOKING TIME: 1–1½ hours

INGREDIENTS FOR 4 SERVINGS:
1 pound (500 g) haricot beans, soaked overnight
4½ pints (2½ litres) water
1 tablespoon (25 g) coarse salt
4 peppercorns
1 large onion, peeled and stuck with a clove
1 large carrot, peeled and cut in half lengthwise
2 *bouquets garnis*, made of thyme, bay leaf, and parsley tied together
4 large tomatoes, peeled and chopped
Salt, pepper
1½ ounces (40 g) butter

Place the beans in fresh cold water, bring to the boil, then add the peppercorns, onion, carrot, and 1 *bouquet garni*. Simmer for 1 hour, then add the salt and test to see if the beans are ready. They must be cooked until thoroughly softened. When done, drain them, and discard the *bouquet garni*, onion and carrot.

While the beans are cooking, make a tomato sauce. Place the tomatoes (without any butter or oil) in a saucepan. Add salt, pepper, and the second *bouquet garni*, and cook until the water from the tomatoes has evaporated and a thick sauce is formed (about 30 minutes). Discard the *bouquet garni*. When both the beans and the tomato sauce are done, melt the butter in a large frying pan. Add the beans and tomato sauce, shake the pan (or stir gently) to combine, then serve in a hot dish.

SUGAR PEAS
Pois gourmands

PREPARATION TIME: 10 minutes
COOKING TIME: 30 minutes

INGREDIENTS FOR 4 SERVINGS:
1¾ pounds (800 g) sugar peas (*mange tout*)
4 ounces (125 g) lean bacon, diced
2 ounces (60 g) butter
8 baby onions
1 sprig thyme
Salt, pepper

String the sugar peas and rinse quickly in cold water.

Fry the bacon in a frying pan (no fat is needed) until it begins to brown.

In a separate frying pan, melt the butter and lightly brown the onions, then add the bacon, thyme, and peas. Cover and cook for 30 minutes over very low heat, stirring occasionally. Taste for salt and pepper, then serve in a warm vegetable dish.

Serving suggestion: Serve with Calf's Liver (p. 163).

GLAZED ONIONS
Oignons glacés

PREPARATION TIME: 10 minutes
COOKING TIME: about 15 minutes

INGREDIENTS FOR 4 SERVINGS:
2 bunches of spring onions, or 1 pound (500 g) baby onions
2 ounces (50 g) butter, cut into tiny pieces
1 dessertspoon (15 g) granulated sugar
Salt, pepper

Peel the onions, leaving them whole, wash in cold water, and dry.

Place them in a frying pan large enough to hold them all on the bottom, and add half the butter, the sugar, salt and pepper. Cook over low heat until the onions start to brown, then pour in just enough water barely to cover them (they should not float). Cover the pan and raise the heat; boil for about 10 to 15 minutes over moderate heat, or until all the water has evaporated. When the onions are done, there should be a thick syrup remaining in the pan; shake the pan to glaze the onions by rolling them in the syrup. Add the remaining butter, and season again if necessary.

Serving suggestion: Serve with meat or poultry.

SPLIT PEA PURÉE
Purée de pois cassés

PREPARATION TIME: about 15 minutes (plus soaking time)
COOKING TIME: about 2 hours

INGREDIENTS FOR 4 SERVINGS:
1 pound (500 g) split peas, soaked overnight
Bouquet garni, made of thyme, bay leaf and parsley tied together
3 baby onions, peeled
Salt, pepper
2 tablespoons double cream

Drain the peas, place them in a pot, and add enough fresh cold water barely to cover. Add the *bouquet garni*, onions, salt, and pepper. Bring to the boil, then lower the heat and simmer for about 2 hours. Heat extra water and add it to the pot whenever necessary to keep the peas moist. Stir the peas frequently as they cook to make sure they don't stick to the bottom of the pot. By the time they are done, they should have formed a thick smooth purée, rather like mashed potatoes. Just before serving, stir in the cream and season generously with pepper. Serve in a hot dish.

Serving suggestions: Split peas are the perfect accompaniment to roast pork or sausages (stir the pan juices into the purée before serving).

POTATOES BARBOTON
Barboton de pommes de terre

PREPARATION TIME: 15 minutes
COOKING TIME: 50 minutes

INGREDIENTS FOR 4 SERVINGS:
10 ounces (300 g) salt pork or lean bacon cut into large cubes
8 ounces (250 g) medium onions, peeled and sliced *or* baby onions, peeled
About 18 fluid ounces (50 cl) stock or water
2¼ pounds (1 kg) potatoes, peeled and cut into large cubes *or* new potatoes,
    halved
Bouquet garni made of thyme, bay leaf and parsley tied together
1 clove garlic, peeled and chopped
Salt, pepper
Nutmeg
3 ounces (80 g) softened butter, cut into pieces

Over low heat, cook the salt pork or bacon in a large cast iron pot until it has given out some of its fat and begun to brown. Add the onions and cook for about 5 minutes, being careful not to burn. Add the stock or water, the potatoes, *bouquet garni*, and garlic (the liquid should come about two-thirds of the way up the potatoes). Bring to the boil, season with salt, pepper, and nutmeg, cover the pot and lower the heat. Cook at a gentle boil for 15 minutes, then stir so that the potatoes on top are pushed to the bottom of the pot. Cover and cook 15 minutes more or until the potatoes are tender. Check the level of the liquid – it should come about a third of the way up the potatoes. If there is more, boil rapidly uncovered to reduce to this amount, then remove the pot from the heat and add the butter. Cover again and leave for 10 minutes off of the heat, then shake the pot to combine the butter with the liquid and serve in the pot or in a serving dish.

Serving suggestions: The potatoes can be cooked in advance and reheated – they are even better (in any case, don't add the butter until 10 minutes before serving, as described).
 This is excellent with Roast Shoulder of Lamb (p. 133).

POTATOES WITH CHIVE SAUCE
Pommes de terre en robe des champs

PREPARATION TIME: 15 minutes
COOKING TIME: about 30 minutes

INGREDIENTS FOR 5 TO 6 SERVINGS:
5 or 6 large potatoes, scrubbed
Salt, pepper
7 ounces (200 g) cream cheese
6 tablespoons (10 cl) double cream
3 tablespoons finely chopped chives
Toasted wholemeal bread (optional)

Before cooking, prick each potato in several places with a needle to keep the skin from breaking open. Place them in a large saucepan, cover with lots of cold water, add a little salt, and bring to the boil. Cook for 30 minutes.

Meanwhile, make a sauce by beating together the cream cheese and cream. Gently stir in the chives, salt, and pepper; chill.

Once the potatoes are done, drain them and place them on a serving platter lined with a clean napkin. Serve the sauce in a sauceboat and slices of toasted wholemeal bread on the side.

SAUTÉ POTATOES
Pommes de terre sautées

PREPARATION TIME: 15 minutes
COOKING TIME: about 20 minutes

INGREDIENTS FOR 4 TO 5 SERVINGS:
1¾ pounds (800 g) new potatoes, *or* 2¼ pounds (1 kg) old potatoes
1 tablespoon olive oil
1½ ounces (40 g) butter
¼ teaspoon dried thyme (or more, to taste)
1 clove garlic, whole and unpeeled
Salt, pepper

It is preferable to use new potatoes for this recipe; their skins can be scraped off with a knife rather than peeled off with a vegetable peeler. If they are very small, they can be left whole or cut in half lengthwise. If you are using old potatoes, peel them, cut them in half, then cut them into slices ½ inch (1 cm) thick. In either case, wash the potatoes in cold water after peeling and dry in a tea-towel.

Heat the oil and butter in a large frying pan. When it starts to foam, add the potatoes, thyme, and garlic. Cook over moderate heat for about 15 to 20 minutes, or until tender, shaking the pan frequently to brown the potatoes evenly and avoid sticking. When the potatoes are done, season with salt and pepper, and serve immediately.

BAKED POTATOES WITH TOMATOES
Pommes boulangère

PREPARATION TIME: 10 minutes
COOKING TIME: 45 minutes to 1 hour

INGREDIENTS FOR 4 SERVINGS:
2¼ pounds (1 kg) old potatoes
1 pound (500 g) tomatoes, peeled and chopped
4 ounces (125 g) bacon, diced
1 teaspoon thyme leaves
¼ bay leaf, crushed or crumbled
Salt, pepper
2 ounces (50 g) butter, cut into little pieces
About 9 fluid ounces (25 cl) water

Preheat the oven to 425°F (220°C or Mark 7).
   Brown the bacon in a frying pan without added fat.
   Peel the potatoes, wash them, and cut them into fairly thin slices. Lightly butter a baking dish just large enough to hold the potatoes, then cover the bottom with a thin layer of potatoes. Sprinkle over some of the tomato, bacon, thyme, bay leaf, salt, pepper, and a little butter. Cover this with a second layer of potatoes, and season them in the same way as the first. Fill the dish in this manner, layer after layer, then pour in enough water to come about halfway up the potatoes. Heat the dish on top of the stove until the water boils, then place in the oven and bake for 45 minutes to 1 hour, or until the potatoes are tender and the top layer has begun to brown.
   Serve in the baking dish.

MASHED POTATOES
Purée de pommes de terre

PREPARATION TIME: 10 minutes
COOKING TIME: about 30 minutes

INGREDIENTS FOR 4 SERVINGS:
2¼ pounds (1 kg) old potatoes
8 to 12 fluid ounces (25 to 35 cl) hot milk
2 tablespoons double cream (optional)
2 ounces (50 g) butter
Salt
Nutmeg

Peel the potatoes and rinse them off quickly under cold running water. Boil them in a large pot of lightly salted water for 20 to 30 minutes (the point of a knife should pierce them easily when done). While the potatoes are cooking, heat the milk.

Drain the potatoes and purée them in a vegetable mill or use a potato masher. Put them in a clean saucepan and whisk in the milk little by little (the amount you use will vary depending on the type of potato you use and how stiff or creamy you like them). Whisk to make a thick, smooth purée. Just before serving, stir in the cream if using, the butter, salt, and nutmeg. Serve immediately.

Serving suggestions: Mashed potatoes should never be prepared in advance and reheated but mashed and seasoned just before serving. Use any leftovers to make other dishes such as Mashed Potato Pancakes (p. 208), French Shepherd's Pie (p. 212), Potato Soufflé (p. 206), etc.

POTATO CRÊPE
Crique

PREPARATION TIME: about 15 minutes
COOKING TIME: 15–20 minutes

INGREDIENTS FOR 2 TO 3 SERVINGS:
1 pound (500 g) old potatoes
1 egg
Salt, pepper
3 tablespoons olive oil

Wash the potatoes, wipe them dry, and peel them (do *not* wash after peeling but wipe them with a clean cloth if necessary). Grate the potatoes coarsely, place them in a bowl with the egg, salt, and pepper, and mix well. All this should be done just before cooking.

Heat 2 tablespoons of the oil in a large frying pan (preferably cast iron). When very hot, add all the grated potatoes and spread them out with the prongs of a fork, pressing down on them lightly to make a large crêpe, or pancake, of even thickness. Cook over moderately high heat for 8 to 10 minutes, or until the underside has browned, then slide the crêpe out into a large plate.

Place the remaining tablespoon of oil in the pan, then place a second plate on top of the crêpe and turn it upside down. Lift off the first plate and slide the crêpe back into the pan to finish cooking 8 to 10 minutes on the second side.

Serve immediately.

Serving suggestions: Serve as a garnish with meat or as a light lunch, accompanied by a Green Salad (p. 66) flavoured with a little garlic, if you like it, and an Oil and Vinegar Dressing (p. 92) made with olive oil and seasoned with finely chopped fresh herbs (parsley, chervil, chives, tarragon, etc.), depending on what's in season.

POTATO SOUFFLÉ
Soufflé de pommes de terre

PREPARATION TIME: 20 to 30 minutes
COOKING TIME: 1 hour 10 minutes

INGREDIENTS FOR 4 SERVINGS:
1¾ pounds (800 g) old potatoes, peeled
7 fluid ounces (20 cl) cold milk
1 tablespoon double cream
1 ounce (30 g) butter
4 eggs, separated
Salt, pepper
4 ounces (125 g) grated gruyère cheese (optional)
3 ounces (75 g) butter (for the mould)

Preheat the oven to 350°F (180°C or Mark 4).

Boil the potatoes in a large pan of lightly salted water for 30 minutes, then drain and purée in a food mill or mash them until smooth. Place them in a large bowl, then stir in the milk, cream, 1 ounce (30 g) butter, egg yolks, salt, pepper and cheese (if using).

Put 3 ounces (75 g) butter in a 7 inch (18 cm) soufflé mould and place in the oven until the butter has melted. Remove from the oven and turn to coat the sides with butter.

In a large mixing bowl, beat the egg whites until stiff, then fold them into the potatoes. Pour the mixture into the mould and place immediately in the oven to bake for 40 minutes. Do not open the oven door while the soufflé is baking, but if possible check to see if it has browned by looking through the window in the oven door. Serve immediately when done.

MASHED POTATO PANCAKES
Galettes de pommes de terre

PREPARATION TIME: 10 minutes
COOKING TIME: 15 minutes per pancake

INGREDIENTS FOR 4 SERVINGS:
10 ounces (300 g) leftover Mashed Potatoes (p. 204)
1 tablespoon flour
2 tablespoons milk
1 egg
1 ounce (30 g) butter
Salt and pepper, or sugar

It is preferable to use 4 little frying pans 5 inches (12 cm) across for cooking the pancakes (see *Note*).

Place the cold mashed potatoes in a mixing bowl and whisk in the flour, milk and egg.

Place a quarter of the butter in each pan and heat until it starts to foam, then spoon a quarter of the potato mixture into it, spreading it out evenly. Cook over moderate heat for 7 minutes, then turn over and finish cooking for 7 minutes (use two plates to turn the pancakes over, as described in the recipe for Potato Crêpe, p. 205). Add a little more butter to the pans if needed when you turn the pancakes over.

Serve the pancakes as soon as they are done. Sprinkle with salt and pepper, or with sugar if you want to use them as a dessert (children like them that way).

COMMENT: You can make one large potato pancake instead of 4 small ones, but it's much harder to turn over.

Note: if you don't have 4 small frying pans, form 4 potato pancakes with your hands and cook them in a large pan. In this case turn them over with a fish slice. Ed.

POTATOES AU GRATIN
Gratin de pommes de terre au lait

PREPARATION TIME: 20 minutes
COOKING TIME: 45 minutes

INGREDIENTS FOR 4 SERVINGS:
2¼ pounds (1 kg) potatoes
1 pint (60 cl) milk
Nutmeg
Salt, pepper
1 clove garlic, peeled and split lengthwise
4 ounces (125 g) grated gruyère cheese
3 tablespoons double cream
1 ounce (30 g) butter, cut into small pieces

Preheat the oven to 350°F (180°C or Mark 4).

Peel the potatoes and wash quickly in cold running water, then wipe dry.

Cut them into slices about ¼ inch (5 mm) thick and reserve.

Bring the milk to the boil in a large saucepan, add the potatoes, a little nutmeg, and season with salt and pepper. Shake the pan gently to make the potatoes settle into the milk (they should be barely covered; if not, add a little warm water). Lower the heat and simmer, uncovered, over very low heat for 20 to 25 minutes, or until tender.

Rub a baking dish (preferably porcelain or earthenware) with the garlic.

When the potatoes are done, lift some out of the milk with a slotted spoon and place them on the bottom of the baking dish. Sprinkle with a little grated cheese, add another layer of potatoes, sprinkle with cheese, and continue filling the dish, layer by layer, ending with cheese.

Measure the milk remaining from cooking the potatoes; there should be about 5 fluid ounces (15 cl) left. If there is more than that, boil it to reduce to this amount, then pour it over the potatoes. Spoon in the cream, dot the surface with butter, then place the dish in the oven and bake for 20 minutes, or until the surface is golden brown.

BAYALDI

PREPARATION TIME: 20 minutes
COOKING TIME: about 50 minutes

INGREDIENTS FOR 4 TO 6 SERVINGS:
4 medium courgettes about 1½ pounds (700 g)
2 small aubergines about 1¼ pounds (600 g)
8 ounces (250 g) onions
1¼ pounds (600 g) tomatoes
1 clove garlic, peeled and crushed
½ teaspoon dried thyme
½ bay leaf, crumbled
Salt, pepper
3 ounces (80 g) butter cut into small pieces
3½ ounces (100 g) grated gruyère cheese (see *Note*)

Preheat the oven to 350°F (180°C or Mark 4).

Wash the vegetables and wipe them dry, then cut them into slices about ½ inch (1 cm) thick (if using a large aubergine rather than 2 smaller ones, cut it in half lengthwise before slicing). Keep all the vegetables separate from each other.

Butter a large baking dish (preferably earthenware or enamelled cast iron). Cover the bottom of the dish with the onions, then make a layer of courgettes and sprinkle with a little of the garlic, thyme, bay leaf, salt and pepper. Next make a layer of aubergine and lastly a layer of tomato, seasoning each layer as you did the courgettes. Dot the surface with half the butter, then place in the oven for 30 minutes. At the end of this time, sprinkle with the cheese, dot with the remaining butter, and bake 20 to 30 minutes more or until golden brown on top. (If the vegetables dry out during the first 30 minutes' baking, cover them with aluminium foil; remove the foil for only the last 10 minutes of the baking time.)

Serving suggestion: Serve with roast or boiled meat.

Note: If preferred, the cheese can be omitted and 4 tablespoons (8 cl) of olive oil used instead of butter. In this case, pour all the oil over the surface of the vegetables before putting them in the oven.

Instead of making layers as described here, you can simply make parallel lines of overlapping vegetables as shown in the photo, and bake them in individual baking dishes rather than in one large one. Ed.

FRENCH SHEPHERD'S PIE
Hachis parmentier

PREPARATION TIME: 20 to 30 minutes
COOKING TIME: 1 hour 15 minutes

INGREDIENTS FOR 4 SERVINGS:
2¼ pounds (1 kg) old potatoes, peeled
10 fluid ounces (35 cl) milk
1 egg
2 ounces (50 g) grated gruyère cheese
Salt, pepper
Nutmeg
10 ounces (300 g) leftover cooked meat or poultry, or a mixture of both,
    chopped
2 medium onions, peeled and chopped
1 tablespoon tomato purée
2 ounces (50 g) softened butter, cut into pieces

Boil the potatoes in lightly salted water for 30 minutes, then drain and purée in a food mill or mash until smooth. Add the milk, then beat in the egg, cheese and a little salt, pepper and nutmeg. Reserve.

Preheat the oven to 350°F (180°C or Mark 4).

Place the chopped meat, onions, tomato purée, salt and pepper in a mixing bowl. Beat together with a wooden spoon and reserve.

Butter a baking dish (preferably porcelain or enamelled cast iron). Spread half the mashed potatoes evenly over the bottom in a thick layer, then pour in the meat mixture and spread it out evenly over the potatoes. Pour in the remaining potatoes and use a fork to spread them over the meat and to decorate the surface by making lines and patterns over it. Dot the surface with the butter (see Variations), then place in the oven and bake for 45 minutes or until brown on top.

Serve hot from the oven in the baking dish.

Serving suggestion: This dish is a meal itself; serve it with a Green Salad (p. 66).

VARIATIONS: If you like, home-made Tomato Sauce (p. 90) or grated gruyère cheese can be spread over the surface of the potatoes instead of butter before baking.

BAKED PUMPKIN FLAN
Flan au potiron

PREPARATION TIME: 20 minutes
COOKING TIME: 55 minutes

INGREDIENTS FOR 3 TO 4 SERVINGS:
2¼ pounds (1 kg) fresh pumpkin
1 tablespoon cornflour
9 fluid ounces (25 cl) milk
6 tablespoons (10 cl) double cream
2 eggs
Salt, pepper
Nutmeg

Peel the pumpkin and remove the seeds. Cut it into large cubes, then drop them into a pot of boiling salted water and cook at a moderate boil for 20 minutes. Drain in a colander (leave it in the colander for 5 to 10 minutes so that the maximum amount of water will drain off).

Purée the pumpkin in a food mill, blender, or food processor and reserve.

Preheat the oven to 425°F (220°C or Mark 7).

Mix the cornflour with a little cold water. Boil the milk and stir in the cornflour mixture. Remove from the heat and add first the cream, then the eggs, beating constantly. Stir in the pumpkin, then season with salt, pepper and a little nutmeg.

Lightly butter a small baking dish and pour in the pumpkin mixture, spreading it evenly around the dish. Place in the oven and bake for about 35 minutes or until golden brown on top.

Serve hot from the oven in the baking dish.

VARIATIONS: You can make a pumpkin dessert by adding 2 ounces (50 g) of granulated sugar and a little vanilla extract to flavour the pumpkin instead of salt, pepper and nutmeg.

RATATOUILLE

PREPARATION TIME: 30 minutes
COOKING TIME: 1½ hours

INGREDIENTS FOR 4 SERVINGS:
1 pound (500 g) aubergines, peeled and diced
Salt, pepper
1¾ pounds (800 g) tomatoes, peeled and chopped
Bouquet garni, made with thyme and bay leaf tied together
1 or 2 cloves garlic, peeled
3 tablespoons olive oil
1 pound (500 g) onions, peeled and sliced
8 ounces (250 g) carrots, peeled and cut into thin sticks
1¾ pound (800 g) courgettes, diced

Place the aubergines in a mixing bowl and sprinkle generously with salt; leave for 30 minutes before cooking. When the time is up, press them between the palms of your hands to squeeze out all their water before mixing them with the other vegetables.

Place the tomatoes in a saucepan with the *bouquet garni* and garlic (no oil or butter), and simmer uncovered for at least 30 minutes to make a thick sauce.

Meanwhile, heat the oil in a large pot, add the onions and carrots, and brown lightly. Add the courgettes, cover and simmer for 15 minutes, stirring occasionally; then add the aubergines and the tomato sauce, which should be cooked by then. Season with salt and pepper, cover once more, and simmer for 1 hour, stirring from time to time.

Serve on a hot platter or in the pot it was cooked in (especially if you used an earthenware one).

Note: Ratatouille is also excellent cold. Ed.

10

PASTA AND RICE

Pasta and rice can be served with many main dishes, and are excellent accompaniments to either fish or meat when well prepared.

PASTA CRÊPE
Galette de nouilles

PREPARATION TIME: 10 minutes
COOKING TIME: 15 minutes

INGREDIENTS FOR 2 SERVINGS:
7 ounces (200 g) leftover cooked pasta (*tagliatelli*)
1 egg
1 tablespoon double cream
Salt, pepper
1 ounce (30 g) butter

Place the leftover pasta in a mixing bowl; separate the pieces with your fingers if they are stuck together. Add the egg, cream, salt, and pepper. Stir gently to mix, being careful to break the pasta as little as possible.

Melt half the butter in a frying pan. When it starts to foam, pour in the pasta, spread it out with a fork to flatten it into a sort of pancake, and cook for about 7 minutes. When brown on the first side, turn the pancake over using two plates as described in the recipe for Potato Crêpe (p. 205). Add the remaining butter to the pan and slide the pancake back in. Cook for 7 minutes on the second side, then slide onto a serving platter and serve immediately.

PASTA PROVENÇALE-STYLE
Pâtes à la provençale

PREPARATION TIME: 15 minutes
COOKING TIME: 30 minutes

INGREDIENTS FOR 4 SERVINGS:
1 pound (500 g) tomatoes, peeled and chopped
1 clove garlic, peeled
Bouquet garni, made with thyme and bay leaf
1 ounce (30 g) butter
1 tablespoon olive oil
1 medium onion, peeled and sliced
4 ounces (125 g) bacon, diced
Salt, pepper
About 1¼ pound (600 g) fresh pasta (see Comment and Variation, p. 218)
Grated Parmesan cheese

First make the sauce. Place the tomatoes, garlic, and *bouquet garni* in a saucepan and bring to the boil. Lower the heat and simmer for 15 minutes, stirring frequently.

Meanwhile, heat the butter and oil in a frying pan, add the onion and bacon, and cook to brown lightly. When the tomatoes are cooked, stir them into the pan, season with salt and pepper, and simmer for 15 minutes more, stirring occasionally. When the sauce is done, remove the *bouquet garni* and discard.

Cook the pasta in rapidly boiling salted water for 2 to 7 minutes (see Pasta with Cream and Basil Sauce, p. 218). Drain, put the pasta in a large, hot serving dish, stir in the sauce, and serve, with a bowl of grated Parmesan on the side.

PASTA PANCAKE
Pain de nouilles

PREPARATION TIME: 10 minutes
COOKING TIME: 10 minutes

INGREDIENTS FOR 4 SERVINGS:
14 ounces (400 g) leftover cooked pasta (preferably *tagliatelli*)
Salt, pepper
2 eggs
3 tablespoons chopped chives, basil, or parsley
2 ounces (50 g) butter

Place the noodles in a bowl and separate them with your fingers. Season with salt and pepper, then stir in the eggs and the herb of your choice.

Melt the butter in a large frying pan; when very hot, pour in the noodle mixture and spread it out into a large pancake using a fork. Cook for 5 minutes or until brown, then turn over using two plates, as described in the recipe for Potato Crêpe, p. 205. Cook for about 5 minutes on the second side, then slide out of the pan and on to a hot serving platter. Serve immediately.

RICE
Riz créole

PREPARATION TIME: 5 minutes
COOKING TIME: 15 minutes

INGREDIENTS FOR 4 SERVINGS:
2½ pints (1½ litres) water
1 teaspoon salt
8 ounces (250 g) long-grain rice

Bring the water to the boil in a saucepan, add the salt, and stir in the rice. Boil gently, uncovered, for 15 minutes, stirring occasionally; then drain and serve.

Serving suggestions: Serve with butter, salt, and pepper, with a Tomato Sauce (p. 90), or with the meat juices or sauce that goes with the dish it is used to garnish.

PASTA WITH CREAM AND BASIL SAUCE
Pâtes à la crème et au basilic

PREPARATION TIME: 15 minutes
COOKING TIME: about 20 minutes

INGREDIENTS FOR 4 SERVINGS:
5 ounces (150 g) shelled peas – buy 12 ounces (350 g) if in pod
About 1¼ pounds (600 g) fresh pasta (see Comment and Variation)
5 ounces (150 g) prosciutto (Parma ham) or bacon, diced
1 ounce (30 g) butter
6 tablespoons (10 cl) double cream
Salt, pepper
1 tablespoon coarsely chopped fresh basil

Boil the peas in a pot of lightly salted boiling water for 5 to 10 minutes, drain, and reserve.

In a pan large enough to hold the pasta comfortably, but not too large nevertheless, bring lightly salted water to the boil. Add the pasta and cook at a rapid boil for 2 to 7 minutes. Cooking times will vary depending on the pasta used; generally speaking, when all the pasta floats, it's done. In any case, taste one: the pasta should be cooked *al dente*, that is, somewhat firm and *never* mushy.

When the pasta is cooked, drain in a colander and return to the pan over moderate heat. Add the peas, butter and ham, and stir in the cream, salt, pepper, and basil. Heat to warm through, stirring gently, but do not allow the cream to boil. Serve immediately.

COMMENT: If freshly made pasta is unavailable, buy 12 to 14 ounces (350 to 400 g) of egg-enriched pasta. Cooking times vary, so consult instructions given on the package.

VARIATION: You can use *pasta verde* as well as plain ones, as shown in the photo. I suggest cooking them separately but mixing the two together.

BAKED VERMICELLI
Paillasson de vermicelle

PREPARATION TIME: 5 minutes
COOKING TIME: about 20 minutes

INGREDIENTS FOR 4 SERVINGS:
1 ounce (30 g) butter
2 tablespoons olive oil
8 ounces (250 g) vermicelli
1 clove garlic, whole and unpeeled
18 fluid ounces (50 cl) beefstock or bouillon (see French Boiled Dinner,
  p. 118)
Salt, pepper

Preheat the oven to 425°F (220°C or Mark 7).

On top of the stove, heat the butter and olive oil in a medium-sized enamelled cast iron baking dish. Add the vermicelli and garlic and cook for 6 to 7 minutes, stirring and tossing the vermicelli almost constantly to brown them lightly.

Lower the heat and add the stock; simmer for 5 to 6 minutes or until it has completely evaporated. Remove the pan from the heat, sprinkle with salt and pepper, then place in the oven for 10 minutes to finish cooking.

Either serve in the baking dish or turn out by running the tip of a knife all around the edge, placing a large flat platter on top of the dish and flipping everything upside down so the cake of vermicelli is sitting on the platter.

Serve immediately.

Serving suggestion: This is an excellent accompaniment to the Boiled Beef au Gratin (p. 116).

RISOTTO WITH TOMATOES
Risotto à la tomate

PREPARATION TIME: 15 minutes
COOKING TIME: 40 minutes

INGREDIENTS FOR 4 SERVINGS:
1½ pound (700 g) tomatoes, peeled and chopped
5 tablespoons olive oil
4 medium onions, peeled and chopped
18 fluid ounces (50 cl) beef stock or bouillon (see French Boiled Dinner p. 118)
8 ounces (250 g) rice
Salt, pepper
1 pinch saffron (optional)
3 ounces (75 g) grated Parmesan cheese

First cook the tomatoes. Heat 2 tablespoons of the oil in a saucepan, add the onion and cook to brown lightly, then add the tomatoes, stir, and simmer uncovered for 15 to 20 minutes.

When the tomatoes are done cook the rice. Heat the remaining olive oil in a large saucepan. Heat the stock in another saucepan.

When the olive oil is very hot add the rice. Stir for a few seconds or until translucent, then add the tomato sauce and the hot stock. Salt and pepper, add the saffron (if using), stir, then cover the pan and simmer slowly for about 20 minutes. When the rice is done all the liquid should have been absorbed.

Gently stir in the Parmesan, taste for salt and pepper and serve immediately.

Serving suggestion: Risotto is an excellent accompaniment to the French Boiled Dinner p. 118.

MACARONI AU GRATIN
Gratin de macaroni

PREPARATION TIME: 15 minutes
COOKING TIME: about 1 hour 10 minutes

INGREDIENTS FOR 6 SERVINGS:
1 pound (500 g) long macaroni
1 clove garlic, peeled and split lengthwise
2¼ pints (1¼ litres) milk
Salt, pepper
Nutmeg
Generous 7 fluid ounces (20 cl) double cream
4 ounces (125 g) grated gruyère cheese
2 ounces (50 g) butter, cut into small pieces

Preheat the oven to 350°F (180°C or Mark 4).

Cook the macaroni in rapidly boiling salted water for 7 minutes, then drain in a colander (do not cool).

Rub a large baking dish with the pieces of garlic and butter it well.

Heat the milk in a large saucepan and season generously with salt, pepper, and nutmeg. Stir in the cream and the macaroni, then pour into the baking dish. Sprinkle with the grated cheese, dot with butter, and bake for 1 hour (the macaroni should bake for a long time; it will finish cooking in the milk and become beautifully browned on top).

RICE PILAF
Riz pilaf

PREPARATION TIME: 5 minutes
COOKING TIME: 20 minutes

INGREDIENTS FOR 4 SERVINGS:
1¼ pints (75 cl) stock or water
2 ounces (60 g) butter
1 onion, peeled and finely chopped
8 ounces (250 g) long-grain rice
Salt, pepper
3½ ounces (100 g) grated gruyère cheese

Heat the stock or water in a saucepan.

Melt the butter in a second saucepan and lightly brown the onion, then stir in the rice. Use a ladle to add enough of the stock or water barely to cover the rice, salt lightly, stir, and boil gently, uncovered, until the liquid has been absorbed (about 5 minutes). Add half the remaining liquid; when this has been absorbed add the rest. Cook the rice for a total of about 20 minutes; when done all the liquid should have evaporated.

Season with salt and pepper to taste, then serve, with a bowl of freshly grated cheese on the side.

Serving suggestion: Rice pilaf can be served with many meat and fish dishes.

11

DESSERTS

Most of these desserts are traditional family fare in France – everyone's favourites.

APPLE PURÉE
Compote de pommes

PREPARATION TIME: 10 minutes
COOKING TIME: 20 minutes

INGREDIENTS FOR 4 SERVINGS:
2¼ pounds (1 kg) dessert apples
4 tablespoons water
2 ounces (50 g) castor sugar
1 pinch cinnamon, and lemon juice to taste
3½ ounces (100 g) light brown sugar and 2 tablespoons water

Peel, quarter and seed the apples, then cut into thin slices. Place in a saucepan with the water and sugar and simmer uncovered for 20 minutes, stirring occasionally. Beat vigorously (preferably with a wire whisk) to purée.

You can either flavour the apple purée with cinnamon and lemon juice, or with caramel. In the second case, make a caramel by cooking the brown sugar and water together until the mixture darkens and caramelizes. Stir the hot apple purée into the caramel and serve warm.

CHERRY CLAFOUTIS
Clafoutis

PREPARATION TIME: 20 minutes
COOKING TIME: ¾ to 1 hour

INGREDIENTS FOR 6 SERVINGS:
1 pound (500 g) dark, ripe cherries
½ teaspoon baking powder
8 ounces (250 g) flour
3 eggs
2 ounces (50 g) castor sugar
4 fluid ounces (12 cl) milk
1 pinch salt
1 ounce (30 g) butter (for the pan)
Sugar (to finish)

Preheat the oven to 350°F (180°C or Mark 4).

Wash the cherries, dry them in a clean cloth and remove the stems, but do not stone them. Reserve.

Mix the baking powder and flour together in a bowl, then push it up against the sides of the bowl to form a well in the centre. Break the eggs into the well, add the sugar, milk and salt; stir, mixing the flour in as it falls from the sides. The finished batter should be smooth; if there are any lumps work the batter through a sieve to eliminate them.

Butter a 10-inch (25-cm) flan dish (preferably porcelain). Stir the cherries into the batter, then pour it into the dish and bake for 45 minutes to 1 hour. When golden brown remove the clafoutis from the oven and sprinkle with sugar.

Serve either hot or cold in the dish.

CREAM CHEESE LYONS-STYLE
Cervelle des canuts

PREPARATION TIME: 15 minutes (plus 2 hours refrigeration)

INGREDIENTS FOR 4 SERVINGS:
7 ounces (200 g) fresh cream cheese
6 tablespoons (10 cl) double cream
2 tablespoons olive oil
1½ teaspoons red wine vinegar
1 clove garlic, peeled and finely chopped
1 shallot, peeled and finely chopped
Salt, pepper
1 tablespoon finely chopped chervil
1 tablespoon finely chopped chives
1 tablespoon finely chopped parsley
½ tablespoon finely chopped tarragon
Radishes

This is not a dessert, but I didn't really know where else to put it in the book. It's a speciality of Lyons which we eat either as a starter before dinner, or after the main dish (before dessert), or simply as a snack. It can also be served with drinks or as part of the Lyons-style brunch (*mâchon*).

To make it simply beat together the cheese and cream until smooth, then beat or whisk in the oil, vinegar, garlic and shallot. Season with salt and pepper, then stir in the fresh herbs (if you want you can add more herbs to taste).

Refrigerate for at least 2 hours before serving.

Serve cold with pieces of toast and radishes.

STEWED DRIED FRUIT
Compote de fruits secs

PREPARATION TIME: 10 minutes (after overnight soaking)
COOKING TIME: 20 to 30 minutes

INGREDIENTS FOR 4 SERVINGS:
7 ounces (200 g) dried apricots
5 ounces (150 g) dried figs
4 ounces (125 g) prunes
4 ounces (125 g) dried bananas
10 hazelnuts
10 almonds

Place all the fruit in a bowl, cover with cold water and leave overnight to swell up. Next day, strain off the soaking water, place the fruit in a large saucepan and cover with fresh water. Bring just to the boil, then immediately lower the heat, cover, and simmer slowly for 20 to 30 minutes or until very tender. Pour into a salad bowl and leave to cool completely, then chill for at least an hour in the refrigerator.

Just before serving, stir in the nuts.

Serving suggestion: Serve with Madeleines (p. 246).

CUSTARD SAUCE
Crème anglaise

PREPARATION TIME: about 30 minutes
COOKING TIME: about 20 minutes

INGREDIENTS FOR 6 SERVINGS:
1 vanilla pod
18 fluid ounces (50 cl) milk
3 eggs
3½ ounces (100 g) castor sugar
1 pinch salt

Split open the vanilla pod lengthwise, place in a medium saucepan with the milk and bring just to the boil. Remove the pan from the heat and leave to infuse for 7 to 8 minutes, then remove the vanilla pod.

Away from the heat, in the top of a double boiler, whisk together the eggs, sugar and salt, then whisk in the hot milk. Set the top of the double boiler in place and heat, stirring the mixture constantly for about 8 minutes or until it thickens (it should not boil). Immediately pour the sauce into a serving bowl and allow to cool, stirring occasionally before refrigerating.

Serve cold.

Serving suggestion: Serve with Chocolate Marble Cake, p. 232 (also, see *Note*).

VARIATION: Instead of vanilla, various other flavours can be given to the sauce: for example, stir a little chocolate, coffee, caramel or rum into the sauce after it thickens but before it cools.

Note: Custard sauce is also excellent with fresh fruit such as strawberries, raspberries, pears, etc. Ed.

PANCAKES
Crêpes

PREPARATION TIME: about 10 minutes (plus 1 hour resting time)
COOKING TIME: 5 minutes for each pancake

INGREDIENTS FOR 6 SERVINGS:
2 ounces (50 g) butter
8 ounces (250 g) flour
1 tablespoon castor sugar
1 pinch salt
3 eggs
18 fluid ounces (50 cl) cold milk
Butter or oil (for the pan)

Melt the butter in a small saucepan and reserve.

Place the flour, sugar and salt in a mixing bowl; stir in the eggs, then pour in the milk little by little, stirring at first, then whisking to make a smooth liquid batter. Finally whisk in the melted butter. Leave the batter at room temperature for about 1 hour before making the pancakes.

Lightly butter or oil a frying pan (preferably cast iron or nonstick). When very hot, drop about a tablespoon of the batter into the centre of it, and tip and turn the frying pan to cover the bottom with the batter and make a very thin pancake. Cook for about 2 minutes over moderate heat, turn it over using a flexible-blade spatula, and finish cooking about 3 minutes on the second side. Remove the pancake and lightly butter the pan before cooking the next one.

To keep the pancakes warm after cooking heat a little water to simmering in a saucepan and set a large plate on top. As the pancakes finish cooking put them on the plate and cover with a second plate turned upside down.

Serving suggestions: Serve the pancakes hot with honey, walnuts, jam or chestnut cream.

Note: Pancakes are also delicious simply spread with a little butter and sprinkled with castor sugar and lemon juice. Ed.

CHOCOLATE MARBLE CAKE
Marbré au chocolat

PREPARATION TIME: 20 minutes
COOKING TIME: about 45 minutes

INGREDIENTS FOR 6 SERVINGS:
2 large eggs
4 ounces (120 g) castor sugar
4 ounces (120 g) flour
4 ounces (120 g) butter, well softened but not melted
1 pinch salt
2 ounces (50 g) bitter chocolate
Butter (for the tin)

Preheat the oven to 350°F (180°C or Mark 4).

Beat the eggs and sugar in a mixing bowl until smooth and a pale yellow colour, then sift in the flour, whisking as it is being added. Whisk in the softened butter and the salt; the finished batter should be smooth.

Melt the chocolate in a double boiler.

Lightly butter a small loaf tin or square cake tin, line it with greaseproof paper, then lightly butter the paper as well. Pour the melted chocolate over the batter then barely stir it in, so that there will be light and dark patches. Pour the batter into the tin, smooth the surface and bake for 45 minutes. Test to see if the cake is done by sticking a knife into the centre; it should come out clean and dry. If not, bake the cake a little longer.

Turn the tin upside down on a cake rack to cool as soon as you take the cake from the oven, but don't lift it off the cake until it has cooled completely.

When cool lift off the tin, peel off the paper, turn the cake right side up and place on a serving platter.

This cake will stay fresh up to a week wrapped in aluminium foil.

Serving suggestions: Serve with Custard Sauce (p. 230) or Chocolate Mousse (p. 236) on the side.

APPLE PANCAKE LYONS-STYLE
Matefaim lyonnais

PREPARATION TIME: 20 minutes (plus 3 hours resting time)
COOKING TIME: 30 minutes

INGREDIENTS FOR 4 TO 5 SERVINGS:
7 ounces (200 g) flour
2 eggs
4 ounces (125 g) granulated sugar
½ tablespoon cooking oil
½ teaspoon salt
9 fluid ounces (25 cl) milk
1 tablespoon brandy, *or* 1 teaspoon orange flower water *or* vanilla extract (or more, to taste)
12 ounces (350 g) dessert apples
Oil (for the pan)

The batter must be made 3 hours before cooking. Place the flour and eggs in a mixing bowl, beat with a spoon and add 6 tablespoons of the sugar, the oil and the salt. Continue beating as you pour in the cold milk little by little to make a smooth batter. Add the flavouring of your choice. If there are any lumps in the batter work it through a fine sieve into another mixing bowl. Leave at room temperature for 3 hours.

Just before cooking peel the apples and core them. Chop them coarsely, then stir them into the batter with the remaining sugar. Lightly oil a large frying pan (preferably cast iron or nonstick); when very hot, pour in the batter and spread it out to make a thick pancake. Cook over moderate heat for about 30 minutes, turning over every 6 to 8 minutes (see the Potato Crêpe, p. 205, for instructions on turning over). When the pancake is done a knife stuck into it should come out clean and almost dry.

Serve warm with sugar and cream on the side.

PEARS IN RED WINE
Poires au vin

PREPARATION TIME: 10 minutes
COOKING TIME: 30 minutes (plus cooling time)

INGREDIENTS FOR 4 SERVINGS:
8 very small or 4 medium pears weighing a total of about 2 pounds (900 g)
Juice of ½ lemon
3½ ounces (100 g) castor sugar
9 fluid ounces (25 cl) red wine
½ vanilla pod, split in half lengthwise
1 sprig thyme
2 peppercorns
1 clove
4 tablespoons *crème de cassis* (black currant liqueur)

Preferably use a firm, smooth-skinned variety of pear such as Conference. Small ones need not be peeled (simply rinse them and dry with a cloth); large ones can be peeled, cored, then halved or quartered (see *Note*).

Place the pears in a saucepan just large enough to hold them (stand small pears upright). Add the lemon juice, sugar, red wine, vanilla, thyme, peppercorns, clove and *crème de cassis*. Bring just to the boil, then cover and simmer very slowly for 30 minutes. Lift the pears out of the pan and stand them upright in a serving bowl. Pour the contents of the saucepan over them and leave to cool before serving (several hours will do, but overnight is best). Baste the pears periodically with the wine as they cool, and before serving.

Serving suggestion: Serve with Lyons-style Fritters (p. 250).

Note: Whole pears (even large ones) make for a nicer presentation. Peel them, then place them on their sides in the wine and turn over halfway through the cooking time. When done, stand them upright and baste as described for small pears. Ed.

Pears in Red Wine

CHOCOLATE MOUSSE
Mousse au chocolat

PREPARATION TIME: 15 minutes
COOKING TIME: 10 minutes (plus at least 2 hours refrigeration)

INGREDIENTS FOR 4 SERVINGS:
4 ounces (125 g) semi-sweet chocolate
1 ounce (30 g) softened butter
2 ounces (50 g) castor sugar
4 eggs, separated

Chocolate mousse should be prepared at least 2 hours before serving; ideally it should be made 24 hours ahead of time.

Melt the chocolate and butter in a double boiler over low heat, stirring gently as they begin to melt. Stir in the sugar little by little. When thick and creamy, pour the chocolate mixture into a large mixing bowl and stir until it has cooled to lukewarm, then stir in the egg yolks.

Beat the egg whites until stiff in another mixing bowl, then slide them into the bowl with the chocolate and fold them in, using a wooden spatula or spoon.

When the egg whites have been completely incorporated into the chocolate, place the mousse in the refrigerator for 2 hours or more before serving.

Serving suggestion: Serve with warm Almond Biscuits (p. 256).

MY CHESTNUT PUDDING
Pudding de chez nous

PREPARATION TIME: 20 minutes
COOKING TIME: about 40 minutes

INGREDIENTS FOR 4 SERVINGS:
2 teaspoons softened butter (for the mould)
1 tablespoon castor sugar
8 ounces (250 g) *marrons glacés* (see *Note*)
1½ ounces (40 g) softened butter
3 tablespoons double cream
4 egg yolks
3 egg whites

Bring a large saucepan of water to the boil.

Preheat the oven to 425°F (220°C or Mark 7).

Generously butter a 6-inch (15-cm) charlotte mould or a 7-inch (18-cm) soufflé mould. Sprinkle in the sugar and turn the mould to coat the sides with it. Place the mould in the refrigerator while making the pudding.

Place the chestnuts in a mortar with the butter and pound to a paste, then stir in the cream. Pour the chestnut mixture into a fine sieve and use a wooden spoon to work it through and make a fine, smooth paste. Stir in the egg yolks.

Beat the egg whites until stiff, then fold them into the chestnut cream. When all the egg whites have been added and the mixture is smooth remove the mould from the refrigerator and pour in the chestnut mixture. Place the mould in a roasting pan and pour in enough boiling water to come about a third of the way up the sides of the mould, then place in the oven and bake for 40 minutes. Test to see if the pudding is done by sticking the tip of a knife into it; if it comes out clean and dry the pudding is done. If not it needs to cook longer.

Either turn out the pudding when it comes from the oven and sprinkle with icing sugar, or serve in the mould (in which case it's preferable to bake it in a porcelain soufflé mould). Serve warm but not hot.

Serving suggestion: Serve with Apricot Jam (p. 258) and macaroons.

Note: Marrons glacés are sold at Christmas in France; in the course of being candied, many of them break, and they are sold at much lower prices than the whole ones. It is these broken ones that Paul Bocuse uses in making this dessert, but whole ones can of course be used instead. Ed.

BAKED APPLES
Pommes au four

PREPARATION TIME: 15 minutes
COOKING TIME: 45 minutes

INGREDIENTS FOR 4 SERVINGS:
4 large apples
1 ounce (30 g) butter
4 fluid ounces (12 cl) water
2 ounces (60 g) castor sugar
4 tablespoons raspberry or red currant jelly

Preheat the oven to 350°F (180°C or Mark 4).

Wash the apples and wipe them dry; cut out the stems, but I wouldn't core them since the seeds give a nice taste to them (if you prefer, you can core them, of course). Slit the skin all round each apple with a sharp knife.

Place the apples in a lightly buttered baking dish, put a little of the butter on top of each one, add the water and place in the oven. After 15 minutes, sprinkle each apple with sugar, then return to the oven and bake for 30 minutes more or until tender.

Remove the apples from the oven and allow to cool for 10 to 15 minutes; they should be served warm but not hot. Just before serving spoon a little jelly into each one, and serve in the baking dish.

RICE PUDDING
Riz au lait

PREPARATION TIME: 10 minutes
COOKING TIME: about 50 minutes

INGREDIENTS FOR 4 SERVINGS:
2¼ pints (1 litre) milk
7 ounces (200 g) castor sugar
½ teaspoon salt
1 vanilla pod, split in half lengthwise
7 ounces (200 g) pudding rice

Place the milk, sugar, salt and vanilla pod in a large saucepan and bring to the boil. Sprinkle in the rice, stirring. Lower the heat (use a heat diffuser for very low, even heat), cover the pan and cook the rice for 45 minutes to 1 hour or until it is tender and has absorbed practically all the milk (the milk left over will be absorbed as the rice cools).

Remove the vanilla pod, pour the rice into a bowl, and leave to cool; it can be served either warm or cold.

Serving suggestions: Serve with a homemade jam (Chapter 13), poached fruits or candied fruits.

DRIED APRICOT SOUFFLÉ
Soufflé aux abricots

PREPARATION TIME: 20 minutes
COOKING TIME: 30 minutes

INGREDIENTS FOR 4 SERVINGS:
Softened butter
Castor sugar (for the moulds)
4 ounces (125 g) dried apricots (see *Note*)
2 tablespoons water
2 tablespoons castor sugar
2 egg yolks
4 egg whites

Preheat the oven to 425°F (220°C or Mark 7).

Butter 4 individual soufflé or ramekin dishes about 4 inches (10 cm) wide. Sprinkle sugar into each one and turn to coat the sides with it. Pour out any excess sugar, then place the dishes upside down on a plate in the refrigerator while making the soufflé batter.

Chop the apricots as finely as possible. Place the water and sugar in a small saucepan and bring just to the boil. Remove from the heat and stir in first the apricots, then the egg yolks; pour into a large mixing bowl and reserve.

Whisk the egg whites until stiff, then fold them into the apricot mixture. Pour the soufflé batter into the dishes and bake for 25 to 30 minutes or until golden brown on top (don't open the oven door, but if possible check by looking through the window in it).

Serve immediately, either in the dishes or unmoulded.

Serving suggestion: Serve with black currant jelly and biscuits.

Note: Be sure to use very soft apricots when making this dish. Ed.

FRUIT SALAD
Salade de fruits

PREPARATION TIME: 30 minutes (plus refrigeration)

INGREDIENTS FOR 4 SERVINGS:
2 dessert apples, peeled, cored and quartered
2 pears (not too ripe), peeled, cored and quartered
1 orange
½ grapefruit
½ pineapple
Juice of 1 lemon
3½ ounces (100 g) walnuts, chopped
2 ounces (50 g) castor sugar
2 bananas
sprig of mint

Place the apples and pears in a large salad bowl. Use a knife to cut off the peel (including the white inner skin) of the orange and grapefruit, then cut out the wedges and add them to the bowl, along with any juice they gave out. Cut the skin off the pineapple, cut out the central core, then cut it into wedges and add to the salad. Add the lemon juice, walnuts and sugar. Stir gently, then refrigerate for about 1 hour before serving.

Just before serving, peel and slice the bananas and add them; serve garnished with mint.

Serving suggestion: Serve with Almond Biscuits (p. 256).

VARIATION: All kinds of fruits other than the ones used here can be used in fruit salads; for example strawberries and cherries, tropical fruits such as kiwis or lichees, or fresh grapes, are all excellent additions.

If you like, 3 tablespoons of brandy or a fruit brandy can be added to the salad at the same time as the lemon juice.

PLAIN SOUFFLÉ
Soufflé bonne femme

PREPARATION TIME: 20 minutes
COOKING TIME: 20 minutes

INGREDIENTS FOR 6 SERVINGS:
Softened butter
Castor sugar (for the moulds)
10 fluid ounces (30 cl) milk
3½ ounces (90 g) castor sugar
1 ounce (30 g) flour
1½ ounces (40 g) softened butter
6 egg yolks
9 egg whites
Icing sugar (to sprinkle on top).

Preheat the oven to 425°F (220°C or Mark 7).

Lightly butter 6 individual soufflé dishes about 4 inches (10 cm) wide. Sprinkle in some sugar and turn to coat the sides of the dishes with it. Pour out any excess sugar, then place the dishes upside down on a large platter in the refrigerator while making the soufflé batter.

Reserve 6 tablespoons of the milk and place the remainder in a saucepan with the sugar; bring to the boil. Meanwhile, stir the reserved milk into the flour. Pour the flour mixture into the boiling milk, stirring, then simmer very slowly for 3 minutes, stirring occasionally. Allow to cool for 2 minutes, then place in a mixing bowl and stir in the butter and the egg yolks. Beat the egg whites until stiff, then fold them into the other ingredients. Pour the soufflé batter into the dishes and bake for about 20 minutes. Sprinkle with a little icing sugar as soon as they come from the oven and serve immediately.

VARIATIONS: When adding the egg yolks you can add 2 tablespoons (or more to taste) of rum, brandy, Grand Marnier, or any other alcohol to the batter to flavour it.

Note: This soufflé batter can be made and poured into the dishes up to 20 minutes before baking. Ed.

YOGHURT ICE CREAM
Glace au yaourt

PREPARATION TIME: 45 minutes

INGREDIENTS FOR 6 SERVINGS:
8 egg yolks
4 ounces (125 g) castor sugar
1 pint (50 cl) plain yoghurt
6 tablespoons (10 cl) double cream
2 ounces (50 g) chopped mixed candied fruit

Place the egg yolks in a bowl with the sugar and whisk until the mixture becomes smooth and pale in colour. Stir in the yoghurt, then the cream, and finally the candied fruit. Pour into an ice cream freezer and churn for 30 minutes or until stiff. You can serve the ice cream directly from the freezer (it's best this way), or put it in containers and keep in a deep freeze for later use.

Serving suggestions: Serve with biscuits or wafers and a sauce made with fresh raspberries and a little sugar blended until smooth in a blender or food processor.

12

PASTRIES

French pastries can be very elaborate, but here are a few that are easy to make and very good.

MADELEINES

PREPARATION TIME: 15 minutes
COOKING TIME: 20 minutes

INGREDIENTS FOR 24 LARGE MADELEINES:
5 ounces (150 g) butter
5 ounces (150 g) castor sugar
1 tablespoon orange flower water (see *Note*)
3 eggs
5 ounces (150 g) flour

Preheat the oven to 425°F (220°C or Mark 7).

Melt the butter in a small saucepan and reserve. Place the sugar, orange flower water and eggs in a mixing bowl and beat with a whisk. Whisk in the melted butter, then add the flour little by little, whisking constantly to make a smooth batter.

Lightly butter the moulds or tins, then fill them by about three-quarters with the batter. Bake for 20 minutes or until a rich golden brown, then turn out on to a cake rack and allow to cool before serving.

Note: French madeleines are always baked in elongated, shell-shaped moulds, but ordinary bun tins will serve, especially the kind with a shell pattern stamped on.

Orange flower water can be replaced by a tablespoon of finely grated orange peel or lemon peel if preferred. Ed.

LEMON FLAN
Tarte au citron

PREPARATION TIME: 20 minutes (plus 1 hour resting time)
COOKING TIME: about 55 minutes (plus 3 hours refrigeration)

INGREDIENTS FOR 6 TO 8 SERVINGS:
For the pastry:
8 ounces (250 g) flour
4 ounces (125 g) softened butter, cut into pieces
3 ounces (75 g) castor sugar
1 egg
For the filling:
3½ ounces (100 g) softened butter, cut into pieces
4 ounces (125 g) castor sugar
3 eggs
4 tablespoons (6 cl) double cream
Juice and finely grated zest of 3 lemons

First make the pastry: place the flour, butter, sugar and egg in a large mixing bowl. Use your fingers to "pinch" the ingredients together, working quickly, until a ball of dough is formed. Place it on a lightly floured table or plate, cover and leave for 1 hour before baking.

Preheat the oven to 400°F (200°C or Mark 6).

Lightly butter and flour a 9-inch (23-cm) flan tin, then roll the pastry out into a thin sheet and line the tin. Cut off any excess pastry from around the edges (see *Note*), then prick the bottom in several places with the prongs of a fork. Place a piece of greaseproof paper on top of the pastry; it should be large enough to cover the bottom and sides of the pastry and stick up above the edges of the tin. Press the paper well against the pastry lining the sides of the tin, then fill the tin with uncooked rice, beans or lentils. Place in the oven and bake for 15 minutes, then remove and lower the oven temperature to 325°F (160°C or Mark 3). Carefully lift out the paper containing the rice or beans (save the rice or beans for baking other flans in the same way).

Make the filling by beating together first the butter and sugar. Beat in the eggs and cream, then add the lemon juice and zest. Pour the filling into the flan tin, return to the oven and bake for about 40 minutes or until the filling and crust have begun to brown. Allow to cool completely, then chill in the refrigerator for 3 hours before serving.

Note: Use any leftover pastry to make biscuits: pack it into a ball, roll it out, and cut into any shape you like. Bake for about 20 minutes or until golden brown. Ed.

ALSATIAN-STYLE CAKE
Gâteau alsacien

PREPARATION TIME: 20 minutes
COOKING TIME: 45–50 minutes (plus 30 minutes resting time)

INGREDIENTS FOR 6 SERVINGS:
8 ounces (250 g) white bread or soft dinner rolls, cut into ½-inch (1-cm) cubes
7 fluid ounces (20 cl) milk
1 vanilla pod, cut in half lengthwise
3 ounces (75 g) castor sugar
2 eggs, separated
1 pound (450 g) dessert apples, peeled, cored and sliced
1 tablespoon cherry brandy (Kirsch)
2 tablespoons cinnamon
2 tablespoons breadcrumbs
⅔ ounce (20 g) butter, cut into little pieces

Leave the bread out overnight in a mixing bowl so that it will become stale before using it to make the cake.

Place the milk in a saucepan with the vanilla pod and bring to the boil, then pour on to the bread and leave for 30 minutes.

Preheat the oven to 350°F (180°C or Mark 4).

Remove the vanilla pod from the bowl with the bread and crush the bread to a paste with a fork. Stir in the sugar, then the egg yolks and finally the apples and cherry brandy.

Beat the egg whites until stiff and fold them into the other ingredients. Butter an 8-inch (20-cm) square or 9-inch (23-cm) cake tin and pour in the batter. Mix the cinnamon and breadcrumbs together, then sprinkle over the batter. Dot with the butter, then bake for 40 to 45 minutes or until a knife stuck into the centre comes out clean.

Serve cold.

PLAIN CAKE
Gâteau manqué

PREPARATION TIME: 10 minutes
COOKING TIME: 40 minutes

INGREDIENTS FOR 4 SERVINGS:
3½ ounces (100 g) flour
5 ounces (150 g) castor sugar
2 eggs
4 fluid ounces (12 cl) milk
1 ounce (30 g) butter, cut into pieces
1 ounce (30 g) granulated sugar

Preheat the oven to 450°F (230°C or Mark 8).

Place the flour, sugar, eggs and milk in a bowl and beat to make a smooth batter.

Generously butter an 8-inch (20-cm) cake tin (preferably porcelain), pour in the batter and place immediately in the hot oven. Bake for 20 minutes, then lower the heat to 350°F (180°C or Mark 4), dot with the butter, sprinkle with the granulated sugar and bake for 20 minutes more.

Serve hot or cold, either alone or with Custard Sauce (p. 230).

LYONS-STYLE FRITTERS
Bugnes

PREPARATION TIME: 15 minutes (plus 2 hours resting time)
COOKING TIME: 4 to 6 minutes for each batch

INGREDIENTS FOR ABOUT 8 SERVINGS:
1 pound (500 g) flour
3 eggs
2 ounces (50 g) granulated sugar
½ teaspoon salt
·Generous ¼ teaspoon baking powder
4 ounces (125 g) softened butter, cut into about 20 pieces
2 tablespoons dark rum (optional)
3½ pints (2 litres) oil (for frying)
Icing sugar

These fritters, similar to doughnuts, are a speciality of Lyons. We make them particularly around Mardi Gras – they keep for several days, so we always make plenty of them.

Place the flour in a large bowl and push it up against the sides to make a well in the centre. Put the eggs, sugar, salt, baking powder, butter and rum into the well. Use a spoon to beat the flour in as it falls from the sides of the bowl. Once the dough becomes thick and difficult to stir, use your hands to knead it like bread dough. When the dough is smooth, place it on a lightly floured cutting board or plate, cover and leave for 2 hours before making the fritters.

When ready to cook, heat the oil in a deep fryer.

Spread out some paper towels for draining the fritters.

Line a large basket or bowl with a clean cloth.

On a lightly floured surface, roll out about a third of the dough at a time into a thin sheet. Use a cookie cutter, knife, or pastry wheel to cut the dough into squares, triangles, or any shape you like.

Test the oil to see if it's hot enough by dropping in a little piece of the dough; if it comes back to the surface almost immediately and begins to brown quickly, the oil is ready.

Fry about 6 to 8 fritters at a time, depending on the size of your deep fryer. Fry for about 2 minutes each side or until golden brown, then lift them out and drain on the paper towels; begin cooking more fritters. When the first batch has drained sufficiently, put them in the basket prepared earlier, sprinkle them with icing sugar and fold the cloth over to keep them warm.

The fritters can be served either warm, as soon as the last batch has been fried, or cold, in which case they can be made in advance.

Serving suggestions: Serve with jams or stewed fruits.

CHEESE CAKE
Tarte au fromage blanc

PREPARATION TIME: 30 minutes (plus 1 hour resting time)
COOKING TIME: 50 minutes

INGREDIENTS FOR 5 TO 6 SERVINGS:
For the shortcrust pastry:
6 ounces (150 g) flour
3 ounces (75 g) softened butter, cut into pieces
1 pinch salt
2 tablespoons water
For the filling:
8 ounces (250 g) cream cheese
6 tablespoons (10 cl) double cream
2 eggs
1 egg yolk
3½ ounces (100 g) castor sugar
1 tablespoon flour
¼ teaspoon vanilla essence (or more, to taste)

Make the pastry by placing the flour, butter and salt in a bowl and rubbing them together until a crumbly mixture is formed. Add the water and knead lightly to make a smooth dough. Place on a lightly floured plate, cover and place in the refrigerator for 1 hour before baking.

Preheat the oven to 350°F (180°C or Mark 4).

Place the cheese in a strainer and drain if necessary, then work it through the strainer into a clean bowl to eliminate any lumps. Add the cream and beat until smooth. Beat in the whole eggs, one by one, then the egg yolk. Mix the sugar and flour together, then beat them into the cheese little by little; add the vanilla essence.

Roll out the pastry on a lightly floured table into a thin sheet. Lightly butter an 8-inch (20-cm) flan dish, line it with the dough and prick the bottom all over with a fork. Pour in the cheese filling. Bake for 20 to 25 minutes then lower the oven temperature to 300°F (150°C or Mark 2) and bake for 25 minutes more.

Serve warm.

RHUBARB TART
Tarte à la rhubarbe

PREPARATION TIME: 20 minutes
COOKING TIME: 30 minutes and 50–55 minutes

INGREDIENTS FOR 5 TO 6 SERVINGS:
Pastry from Cheese Cake recipe (p. 252)
2¼ pounds (1 kg) rhubarb
5 ounces (150 g) castor sugar
Butter (for the pie pan)
1 egg yolk
2 ounces (50 g) slivered almonds
1 ounce (20 g) icing sugar.

Make pastry exactly as described in the recipe for Cheese Cake, using the same measurements.

Peel the rhubarb, then cut each stalk into pieces about ½ inch (1 cm) long. Place them in a saucepan with the sugar and leave for 15 minutes or until the rhubarb has given out water and the sugar has dissolved (stir to help dissolve the sugar). Place the saucepan over moderate heat, bring just to a boil, then lower the heat and simmer for 30 minutes, stirring occasionally (the mixture will thicken and darken in colour). Remove from the heat and reserve.

Preheat the oven to 350°F (180°C or Mark 4).

Roll the pastry out into a thin sheet on a lightly floured table. Butter an 8-inch (20-cm) flan dish and line with the pastry. Place a large sheet of greaseproof paper on top of the pastry – it should be large enough to cover the bottom and sides and stick up above the edges of the dish. Press the paper well against the pastry lining the sides of the dish, then fill the dish with uncooked rice, beans or lentils. Brush the edge of the pastry with egg yolk (this will make it brown nicely as it bakes), then place it in the oven and bake for 40 to 45 minutes.

Remove the dish from the oven; carefully lift out the paper containing the rice or beans (save these for future baking).

Pour the stewed rhubarb into the case, sprinkle with the slivered almonds, and return to the oven for 8 to 10 minutes. Remove from the oven and sprinkle with icing sugar.

Serve warm.

APPLE TART
Tarte aux pommes

PREPARATION TIME: 25 minutes (plus 1 hour resting time)
COOKING TIME: about 45 minutes

INGREDIENTS FOR 6 TO 8 SERVINGS:
8 ounces (250 g) flour
4 ounces (125 g) softened butter, cut into pieces
1 pinch salt
3 tablespoons water
1¾ pounds (800 g) dessert apples, peeled, cored, halved and sliced
2 ounces (50 g) granulated sugar
Black currant jelly, or raspberry or apricot jam (optional).

Make the pastry by placing the flour, butter and salt in a large mixing
bowl and rubbing them together until a crumbly mixture is formed. Add
the water and knead lightly to make a smooth dough. Form it into a
ball, wrap in a clean, lightly floured towel and leave for 1 hour before
baking.

Preheat the oven to 350°F (180°C or Mark 4).

Roll the pastry out into a thin sheet on a lightly floured table. Butter
and flour a 10-inch (25-cm) flan tin, then line it with the pastry,
trimming the edges. Prick the bottom in several places with a fork. Lay
in the slices of apple so that they slightly overlap each other; you can
arrange them in concentric circles to make a flower pattern, for example
(see photo). Sprinkle the apples with the sugar and bake for 35 to 40
minutes.

When the tart comes from the oven you can spread a little jam over
the apples if you like.

Serve warm or cold.

*Note: If you do not have a large flan ring this tart can be made without
one, as in the picture. Simply roll out the pastry, place it on a buttered
and floured baking sheet, and crimp the edges a bit with your fingers to
make a slight border before arranging the apples on it. Ed.*

Apple Tart

ALMOND BISCUITS
Tuiles

PREPARATION TIME: 20 minutes
COOKING TIME: 7 minutes maximum for each batch

INGREDIENTS FOR ABOUT 24 BISCUITS:
1 egg yolk
5 ounces (150 g) granulated sugar
2 ounces (50 g) flour
1 pinch salt
4 ounces (120 g) slivered almonds
3 egg whites

Preheat the oven to 350°F (180°C or Mark 4).

In a mixing bowl, beat the egg yolk and sugar until smooth and pale, then stir in the flour, salt and almonds.

In a separate bowl, beat the egg whites until thick and foamy, but not stiff, then pour them into the bowl with the almond mixture. Cut and fold them into the other ingredients.

Generously butter a baking sheet. Place a generous teaspoon of the batter on the sheet and flatten it out completely, spreading out the mixture with the back of the spoon to make a thin disc about 2 inches (5 cm) wide. When the baking sheet is full – leave lots of space between the biscuits – place in the oven and bake for 5 to 6 minutes. When done, the edge of each biscuit will be golden brown, but the centre will remain pale. Remove the biscuits three or four at a time and quickly lay them on a lightly floured rolling pin (leave the baking sheet with the remaining biscuits in the oven with the door ajar). Press the biscuits against the rolling pin and hold them in place for about 15 seconds so that when they cool they will be arched rather than flat.

Note: You will have to bake the biscuits in several batches. Don't make them more than a few hours before you intend to serve them, because they don't keep well. In any case, as soon as they are completely cool place them in an airtight tin. Ed.

13

JAMS AND JELLIES

The best jams and jellies are homemade. Only perfectly ripe, unbruised fruit should be used in making them.

I think the best thing to cook jam in is a large, unlined copper preserving pan. Clean it before using, each time, by putting a handful of coarse salt and a few spoonfuls of vinegar into it, scouring it with this mixture, then rinsing it out with running water (no soap). Aluminium or stainless steel preserving pans may also be used, but they tend to stick more than copper ones.

Cover the jars with transparent jam pot covers secured with rubber bands; or use the original screw-on lids. If the jam is to be kept for a long period lay a waxed paper disc on its surface; this enables any mould that may develop to be lifted cleanly off. Label and date each jar.

STRAWBERRY JAM
Confiture de fraises

PREPARATION TIME: about 15 minutes (plus overnight soaking)
COOKING TIME: 30–40 minutes

INGREDIENTS FOR 8 ONE-POUND (450 G) JARS:
5 pounds (2.2 kg) fresh ripe strawberries
4½ pounds (2 kg) castor sugar

Wash the strawberries and hull them; you need 4½ pounds (2 kg) for making the jam. Place them in a preserving pan, add the sugar and leave overnight before cooking.

Place the pan over high heat and bring to the boil, then boil for about 15 minutes or until it coats a spoon and a drop or two allowed to cool on a clean plate will stick to the plate when turned upside down (see *Note* to Apricot Jam, p. 258).

When the jam is cooked remove from the heat and ladle it into clean jars. Allow to cool completely before covering and storing.

APRICOT JAM
Confiture d'abricots

PREPARATION TIME: 20 minutes
COOKING TIME: about 40 minutes

INGREDIENTS FOR 8 ONE-POUND (450 G) JARS
5 pounds (2.25 kg) ripe fresh apricots
4½ pounds (2 kg) castor sugar
18 fluid ounces (50 cl) water

Wash the fruit in cold water, drain and pat dry in a tea-towel. Cut open each apricot and remove the stone; you need 4½ pounds (2 kg) apricot halves for making the jam. Place half the apricots in a preserving pan, add the sugar and water and bring to the boil, stirring frequently. Once the water boils, add the remaining apricots and boil for 20 minutes or until the jam is bubbling thickly and coats a spoon. The jam has cooked enough when a drop or two allowed to cool on a clean plate will stick to the plate even when turned upside down. When the jam is done remove it from the heat and ladle into clean jars. Allow to cool completely before covering and storing.

Note: Cooking times for jam vary depending on the ripeness of the fruit used. You can use a sugar thermometer to test it: generally when it reaches about 220°F (104°C) it is done. When cooked enough most jams will bead: dropped on to a cold plate, a drop will hold its shape and not collapse; when cool it will wrinkle if pushed with a finger tip. Ed.

1. Black Currant Jelly – 2. Apricot Jam
3. Red Currant Jelly – 4. Raspberry Jam
5. Quince Jelly – 6. Plum Jam
7. Strawberry Jam

RASPBERRY JAM
Confiture de framboises

PREPARATION TIME: 15 minutes
COOKING TIME: about 50 minutes

INGREDIENTS FOR 8 ONE-POUND (450 G) JARS:
4½ pounds (2 kg) fresh ripe raspberries
18 fluid ounces (50 cl) water
4½ pounds (2 kg) castor sugar

Wash the raspberries. Place them in a preserving pan with the water and sugar and bring to a boil, stirring gently. Boil for 30 minutes or until the jam coats a spoon and a drop or two allowed to cool on a clean plate will stick to it when turned upside down (see *Note* to Apricot Jam, p. 258).

When done remove the jam from the heat and ladle into clean jars. Allow to cool completely before covering and storing.

RHUBARB JAM
Confiture de rhubarbe

PREPARATION TIME: 15 minutes
COOKING TIME: about 1 hour

INGREDIENTS FOR 8 ONE-POUND (450 G) JARS:
8¾ pounds (4 kg) rhubarb
Water
Castor sugar
Juice of 1 lemon

Cut the rhubarb into pieces about 2 inches (5 cm) long.

Bring about 3½ pints (2 litres) of water to a boil in a large pot. Add the rhubarb – it's important that the water *just* covers the rhubarb, so if there is too much, ladle it out, and if there is not enough add hot water as needed. Bring back to the boil and boil the rhubarb for 5 to 7 minutes, then drain it in a colander set over a large bowl to catch the water used for cooking.

Quickly rinse the rhubarb under cold running water and drain.

Measure the water used for cooking the rhubarb and place it in a preserving pan. For every 1¾ pints (litre) of water, add 2¼ pounds (1 kg) of sugar to the pan. Boil the water and sugar for about 30 minutes or until it makes a "thread" when a spoon is dipped into it and lifted out (or use a sugar thermometer and cook to 220°F or 104°C). Add the rhubarb and lemon juice (it keeps the jam a nice colour when cooked), and boil for about 40 minutes or until it coats a spoon and a drop or two allowed to cool on a plate will stick to it even turned upside down (see *Note* to Apricot Jam, p. 258).

When done remove the pan from the heat and ladle the jam into clean jars. Allow to cool completely before covering and storing.

TOMATO JAM
Confiture de tomates

PREPARATION TIME: 20 minutes (plus overnight soaking)
COOKING TIME: about 1 hour

INGREDIENTS FOR MAKING 6 ONE-POUND (450 G) JARS:
9 pounds (4 kg) red or green tomatoes
7 pints (4 litres) water
About 4½ pounds (2 kg) castor sugar
Juice of 2 lemons

Either red or green tomatoes, or a mixture of the two may be used in making this jam.

Wash the tomatoes and wipe them dry. Cut out the stems, then dice the tomatoes and reserve.

Bring the water to the boil in a large saucepan or pot, add the tomatoes, bring back to the boil, then drain in a colander. Weigh the tomatoes, then place them in a preserving pan and add a pound (475 g) of sugar for every pound (475 g) of tomatoes. Bring the tomatoes and sugar to a rolling boil, skim, then remove from the heat. Pour into a large mixing bowl and leave overnight before making the jam.

The next day pour the tomato mixture back into the preserving pan and add the lemon juice. Boil gently for 40 minutes, stirring frequently; watch carefully, because this jam sticks to the pan very easily. The jam is done when it is very thick and a drop or two left to cool on a plate sticks to it without running when tipped, or even when turned upside down.

Remove the jam from the heat and ladle it into clean jars. Allow to cool completely before covering and storing.

QUINCE JELLY
Pâte de coings

PREPARATION TIME: 15 minutes
COOKING TIME: 1 hour 20 minutes

INGREDIENTS FOR 10 SERVINGS:
2¼ pounds (1 kg) quinces
About 1½ pounds (700 g) castor sugar
Granulated sugar (to sprinkle over and to serve)

Use only perfectly ripe, unbruised quinces. Peel them and cut the pulp off the hard central core. Place in a preserving pan with just enough water to cover, bring to the boil and boil rapidly for about 20 minutes or until the quinces are very soft and the water has evaporated. Purée the quinces in a food mill, using a fine grill, or in a blender or food processor. Measure the purée and put it back in the preserving pan. For every 8 ounces (250 g) of purée, add 8 ounces (250 g) of castor sugar. Bring to the boil and boil for 40 minutes, or until the jelly is extremely thick, stirring almost constantly; if the jelly splatters while cooking lower the heat.

Pour the jelly into a shallow porcelain pie dish or earthenware platter – it should be no more than 1 inch (2.5 cm) thick.

Preheat the oven to 300°F (150°C or Mark 2).

Sprinkle the surface of the jelly with a little sugar, then place in the oven for 20 minutes to dry out. Remove from the oven and allow to cool completely, then cut the jelly into long bands. Wrap each band in greaseproof or waxed paper and store in a cool, dry place (do not refrigerate), or serve immediately.

To serve cut the bands into squares, roll them in granulated sugar and arrange on a plate or platter.

APPLE JELLY
Pâte de pommes

PREPARATION TIME: 15 minutes (plus 2–3 hours soaking time)
COOKING TIME: 1 hour 20 minutes

INGREDIENTS FOR 10 SERVINGS:
2¼ pounds (1 kg) tart cooking apples
Juice of 1 lemon
About 1½ pounds (700 g) castor sugar
Granulated sugar (to sprinkle over and to serve)

Make sure the apples you use are perfectly ripe and not bruised. Peel and core them, then cut them into 6 to 8 wedges each. Place them in a preserving pan with the lemon juice and just enough water barely to cover. Bring to the boil and boil rapidly for about 20 minutes, or until the apples are very soft and somewhat translucent and the water has evaporated.

Purée the apples in a food mill, using a fine grill, or in a blender or food processor. Measure the purée and place it in a large mixing bowl. For every 8 ounces (250 g) of purée, add 8 ounces (250 g) of castor sugar. Stir the apples and sugar together, then leave for 2 to 3 hours before cooking.

Pour the apples and sugar into a preserving pan and boil for about 40 minutes or until the purée has become very thick, stirring almost constantly (if it splatters while cooking lower the heat). Pour the jelly into a shallow porcelain pie dish or earthenware platter – it should be no more than 1 inch (2.5 cm) thick.

Preheat the oven to 300°F (150°C or Mark 2).

Sprinkle the jelly with a little sugar, then place in the oven for 20 minutes to dry out. Remove from the oven, allow to cool completely, then cut into long bands about 1 inch (2.5 cm) wide. Wrap each band in greaseproof or waxed paper and store in a cool, dry place (do not refrigerate), or serve immediately.

To serve cut the bands into squares, roll in granulated sugar and arrange on a plate or platter.

14

HOT DRINKS

These are the perfect thing to warm you up on a cold winter's night, or when you're coming down with a cold.

GROG

PREPARATION TIME: 10 minutes
COOKING TIME: 5 minutes

INGREDIENTS FOR 2 SERVINGS:
1 lemon
4 sugar lumps
6 tablespoons (10 cl) rum or cognac
9 fluid ounces (30 cl) water

Wash the lemon in warm water and wipe dry. Rub the sugar lumps against the peel to flavour them, then place 2 sugar lumps and 3 tablespoons of rum or cognac into each of two mugs or large, heat-resistant glasses (you will be pouring boiling water into them).

Cut the lemon in half; cut a thin slice from each half and reserve. Squeeze the remaining lemon and pour half the juice into each glass.

Bring the water to the boil in a small saucepan. Place a teaspoon in each glass, add the water, stir, place a slice of lemon in each one and serve immediately.

EGGNOG
Lait de poule

PREPARATION TIME: 5 minutes
COOKING TIME: about 10 minutes

INGREDIENTS FOR 4 SERVINGS:
4 egg yolks
2 ounces (50 g) castor sugar
4 mugs or bowlfuls of milk

Place the egg yolks and sugar in a mixing bowl and whisk lightly to combine. Bring the milk to the boil in a saucepan, then remove from the heat and wait for 5 minutes before adding it to the egg yolks. Whisk in the hot milk little by little, then pour into the mugs or bowls and serve immediately.

Serving suggestions: You can flavour the eggnog, if you like, with a little rum or cognac to taste just before serving; for children, flavour it with a little coffee, chocolate or orange flower water.

Note: In France, eggnog ("hen's milk", if literally translated) is said to be very good for you if you have a bad cold or the flu.

HOT SPICED WINE
Vin chaud

PREPARATION TIME: 10 minutes
COOKING TIME: about 8 minutes

INGREDIENTS FOR 4 SERVINGS:
1¼ pints (75 cl) good red wine
10 sugar lumps
1 large pinch cinnamon
1 clove
1 lemon

Place the wine, sugar, cinnamon and clove in a saucepan and bring to the boil.

While the wine is heating up wash the lemon, dry in a tea-towel, and cut four thin slices from it. Place one slice of lemon in each glass. Squeeze the remaining lemon and add the juice to the pan with the wine. As soon as the wine boils remove the clove, then pour the wine into the glasses and serve.

Hot wine is excellent for you when you feel a cold coming on.

INDEX

270